THE MIGHTY EIGHTH

A GLIMPSE OF THE MEN, MISSIONS & MACHINES OF THE U.S. EIGHTH AIR FORCE 1942-45

THE MILITARY GALLERY COMMEMORATIVE COLLECTION

GRIFFON INTERNATIONAL

THE MIGHTY EIGHTH
A GLIMPSE OF THE MEN, MISSIONS & MACHINES
OF THE U.S. EIGHTH AIR FORCE 1942-45

THE MILITARY GALLERY COMMEMORATIVE COLLECTION

Many of the images featured in this book have been reproduced as limited
edition prints by the Military Gallery.

www.militarygallery.com

ISBN 978-0-9549970-8-3
A GRIFFON INTERNATIONAL BOOK

First published in the United Kingdom in 2021 by Griffon International Limited,
5 Station Approach, Wendover, Buckinghamshire, HP22 6BN

Copyright © Griffon International Limited 2021

MISSION COMPLETED | Robert Taylor

FIGHTER ESCORT | Robert Taylor

Led by Lieutenants Reps Jones and Leo Kearns, P-51 Mustangs of the 77th Fighter Squadron, 20th Fighter Group depart from their base at Kings Cliffe, Northamptonshire, tasked with escorting Eighth Air Force bombers to Germany on the morning of 14 January 1945.

CONTENTS

STRUGGLE FOR SUPREMACY | Robert Taylor

CLEARING SKIES

Robert Taylor

After a brief respite in the freezing weather and with the recent snow beginning to thaw, the B-17 Fortresses of the 100th Bomb Group at Thorpe Abbotts, Norfolk prepare to carry out the Eighth Air Force's latest mission to Germany, during the harsh winter of early 1945.

HOME AT DUSK | Robert Taylor

INTRODUCTION

The heroics of the airmen who served in the United States Eighth Air Force and fought in the embattled skies of Europe during World War Two are legendary. When in 1942 they commenced their campaign against Nazi Germany, their arrival sent a deep shudder of despair through the German High Command. For the next three years, whilst RAF Bomber Command bombed at night, by day the American Eighth Air Force pounded the enemy war machine to its knees until, by May 1945, victory had finally been won.

This historic book provides a unique glimpse into the lives of some of the men and machines that fought in that bitter, often titanic struggle, together with some of the extraordinary missions they flew.

It is also beautifully illustrated using an unparalleled collection of paintings and drawings from the archives of the Military Gallery who, for nearly five decades, have forged unique links with dozens of veterans who flew and fought with the Eighth Air Force. These include the late Lieutenant General James H. Doolittle, one-time Commander of the Eighth Air Force, enabling some of the world's most talented aviation artists to create many of the works featured in these pages.

'Untempered by ideas of caution, the men of the Eighth Air Force pursued their concept of strategic bombing with dogmatic faith. It was this fervour to get things done, to surmount all technical and operational obstacles, that took the Eighth further along the road it chose than ever the British or Germans would have deemed possible.

Procrastination and the negative were scorned, and even bloody experiences did not deter the overwhelming intention to succeed. This spirit percolated from the top to the bottom; each isolated combat group set in the English countryside proclaimed itself "the best damn group in the AAF", and in a sense, it probably was.'

Historian Roger Freeman – The Mighty Eighth

LIGHTNING STRIKE | Robert Taylor

Richard Taylor

PART ONE: 1942

MAJOR GENERAL CARL A. SPAATZ
COMMANDER OF THE EIGHTH AIR FORCE

5 May – 30 November 1942

SEVEN AMERICANS IN LONDON

FRIDAY 20 FEBRUARY 42
RAF HENDON London

A small group of senior RAF officers stood outside a grey, dismal-looking building at Hendon airfield. Huddled against the cold they watched the distant DC-3 as it descended through overcast skies towards the runway in front of them and noted, with an appreciative eye, that the pilot made a near-perfect landing. The weather-beaten aircraft slowed, turned and then lumbered across the damp grass towards the hardstand in front of them. It stopped with a gentle lurch and, as the pilot cut the engines, the deafening roar of the twin Pratt & Whitneys subsided and the propellers slowed to a halt. For the first time in the nine hours since they'd left Lisbon the crew could finally relax.

It had been a long, weary flight. They'd flown as far out into the Bay of Biscay as possible, ever-vigilant of long-range enemy aircraft looking for easy prey. Whilst the neutrality of Portugal was generally observed by both sides it had still been a tense ride – and for good reason: over these same waters another aircraft carrying the great English film star Leslie Howard would later fall to the guns of eight Luftwaffe Ju 88s with the loss of all on board. On this flight, however, the crew had encountered nothing except cloud and turbulence, and the passengers little but a bumpy ride.

Among the latter were seven Americans and, mindful of Portuguese neutrality, for this trip they'd worn civilian clothes. They were, in fact, officers in the United States Army Air Force and, led by Brigadier General Ira C. Eaker the group included Lieutenant Colonel Frank A. Armstrong Jr., Major Peter Beasley, Captains Frederick W. Castle and Beirne Lay Jr., and Lieutenants Harris Hull and William Cowart Jr. They formed the advance party tasked with organising the arrival and build-up in

ARRIVAL AT HENDON | Richard Taylor

Brig-Gen Eaker and his team arrive at RAF Hendon.

Britain of a new air force soon confirmed by name: the 'Eighth' Air Force, whose primary task was dedicated to a wholesale bombing campaign against Germany.

Co-operation between the U.S. Eighth Air Force and the Royal Air Force would be close, with the former drawing heavily upon the procedures of Bomber Command – a force with well over two years' hard-won battle experience. Eaker and his staff, however, were keen to put into practice the USAAF's long-held doctrine of high-altitude daylight bombing about which the British, having suffered heavy losses in their early daylight raids, were sceptical.

The American officers and their staff, initially working alongside their RAF colleagues at RAF Bomber Command headquarters near High Wycombe, soon had their own premises at a new location, courtesy of the British Air Ministry. And, to maintain the close co-operation that was already developing, the site was nearby.

"We won't do much talking until we've done more fighting. After we've gone, we hope you'll be glad we came."
Brigadier General Ira C. Eaker, Jan 1942

FIRST ARRIVALS

15 APRIL 42

DAWS HILL

HIGH WYCOMBE Buckinghamshire

The founder of Wycombe Abbey, a boarding school for girls, had been a formidable woman. Born in 1846, Frances Dove was one of the first women to attend Girton College, Cambridge and the prestigious school that she created in 1896 was located in High Wycombe, close to the headquarters of RAF Bomber Command. Apart from the Abbey house, rebuilt in the gothic style by James Wyatt, there were almost 250 acres of secluded parkland that included Daws Hill, the grand and elegant

one-time home of the Carrington family, the Abbey's original owners.

Although Frances Dove had retired before the First World War one of her founding aims had been to 'foster the understanding of the needs of others'. Little could she have foreseen that the school she'd founded would itself be asked to fulfil that vision. In March 1942, three months before Frances Dove died, the school was given three weeks to move out and find another home – it had been requisitioned by the Air Ministry for 'the needs of others'.

The 'others', in this case, were the Americans and on Wednesday 15 April 1942 Brigadier General Eaker and his staff moved in to Daws Hill House. Although the headquarters staff would transfer to Bushy Park in Richmond, London a few months later when Major General Carl Spaatz arrived to officially take overall command of the Eighth, Wycombe Abbey – known by the code-word 'Pinetree' and operating the largest telephone switchboard in England – would remain as headquarters of VIII Bomber Command until the end of the war.

MONDAY 11 MAY 42
SS ANDES
LIVERPOOL DOCKS England

The first units of personnel assigned to the new Eighth Air Force crossed the Atlantic at the end of April. Embarked on two transports, the first to sail was the elderly *SS Cathay*, a former P&O liner now requisitioned by the British Admiralty and recently converted in Brooklyn into a troopship. Her passengers included the 15th Bomb Squadron, a unit separated from its parent 27th Bomb Group in the Far East and recently engaged in anti-submarine patrols over the coast surrounding New York.

The remainder of this initial contingent, some 1,850 men including the advance parties of the Eighth Air Force Headquarters, Bomber and Fighter Command staff, departed from Boston five days later on 27 April. They were embarked on the *SS Andes*, a much newer, larger and faster ship who would later break several long-distance speed records.

It was no surprise that the fast convoy to which the *SS Andes* was attached arrived in England first, and she docked in a grey and gloomy Liverpool on Monday 11 May, the Headquarters and Command staff travelling immediately to High Wycombe.

The ageing *SS Cathay* and the 15th Bomb Squadron arrived at Newport in South Wales two days later and they too were soon on their way, this time to Grafton Underwood, an RAF airfield just outside Kettering in Northamptonshire.

FIRST ARRIVALS | Richard Taylor

Shadowed by a pair of RAF Hudsons from 206 Squadron, the SS Andes, carrying some 1850 men forming the advance units of the Eighth Air Force Headquarters, Bomber and Fighter Command staff, arrives at Liverpool, 11 May 1942.

SMALL BUT HEROIC BEGINNINGS

MONDAY 29 JUNE 42
SWANTON MORLEY Norfolk

The 15th Bomb Squadron might have been the first USAAF aircrew to arrive in England but they were distinctly unrepresentative of the B-17 Flying Fortress and B-24 Liberator squadrons with which the Eighth would soon be so closely associated. The 15th BS, having trained on twin-engine Douglas A-20 Havoc light bombers, had been sent to the UK to become a night-fighting defence force but, on arrival, this changed. Having no aircraft of their own they were instructed to commence operations alongside 226 Squadron RAF who were equipped with Bostons – the RAF's version of the A-20 Havoc.

Soon after their arrival at Grafton Underwood the 15th BS found themselves on the move again, this time to Molesworth near Cambridge, from where nine four-man crews were detached east to Swanton Morley, the small grass airstrip just outside Norwich that was home to 226 Squadron and from which the Americans underwent a crash-course in RAF flight procedures, including their host's method of operating light bomber low-level attacks.

It took a month, but on Monday 29 June, Captain Charles C. Kegelman, commanding officer of the 15th BS, and his three crew, flew one of 226 Squadron's twelve Bostons to attack marshalling yards at Hazebrouck, an important railway junction 30 miles south of Dunkirk in the Pas-de-Calais. In doing so they became the first members of the USAAF to drop bombs on enemy-occupied Europe.

Captain Kegelman and his crew came through their first combat encounter unscathed but, ironically, it was on this same day that the first USAAF pilot fatality in Europe occurred. It happened at Atcham in Shropshire where the air echelons of the 31st Fighter Group – who would soon become the Eighth's first operational Fighter Group – had started to arrive. First Lieutenant Alfred Giacomini was killed in a crash landing with his newly-acquired Spitfire.

SATURDAY 4 JULY 42
DE KOOY AIRFIELD Holland

There could have been no more auspicious date on which the Eighth's first full-scale operation took place. It was scheduled to be carried out on American Independence Day, a day on which six crews from the 15th BS, in concert with six crews from 226 Squadron RAF, would fly a low-level mission to attack four Luftwaffe airfields in the Netherlands. The importance of the occasion saw both General Eisenhower and British Prime Minister Winston Churchill on hand to offer encouragement and to witness the twelve Bostons depart, all of which bore RAF roundels. General Spaatz, however, remained sceptical, fearing the mission was more of a publicity stunt pushed by the American press as a 'morale booster for the folks back home'.

Split into four flights of three aircraft, each flight would attack a different target and at least one experienced RAF crew would be in each flight. It didn't, however, guarantee success.

Despite flying low over the North Sea to try to avoid detection, two of the groups ran into heavy flak almost immediately after crossing the Dutch coast and, approaching the targets, it got worse. After dropping his bomb load successfully on Bergen/Alkammar airfield, Second Lieutenant William G. Lynn and his American crew were shot down and killed as they tried to clear the target area. Those in the second group failed to find their objective altogether and returned home.

For the two American crews attacking De Kooy airfield it was a similar disaster. Running through a wall of ground fire the leading aircraft and its RAF crew somehow escaped intact but as the second bomber, flown by the 15th's Second Lieutenant Frederick A. Loehrl, neared the target, it too was hit and crashed in flames. The barrage of murderous light flak made unnerving viewing for Captain Kegelman piloting the final Boston but, nevertheless, he pressed on only for his starboard engine to be hit by ground fire, causing the propeller to sheer off. As the aircraft staggered, smoke and flames streamed from the shattered engine housing, and before he knew it the right wing tip had hit the ground – much to the dismay of the rear gunner as the rear of the fuselage scraped along the grass. Kegelman, however, battled manfully to save the crippled aircraft, jettison his bomb load and, against all odds, regained enough control to keep the crippled Boston in the air, despite a further encounter with a nearby flak tower.

Struggling to maintain height, they managed to regain the coast where the flames finally obliged and went out, allowing Kegelman to bring his men safely home.

In addition to the American losses, one RAF Boston also failed to return. Yet despite the casualties, the regulars in 226 Squadron had been highly impressed with the courage and performance of their American colleagues. For his part in the raid Captain Kegelman was awarded the American Distinguished Service Cross – second only to the Medal of Honor – whilst three others received the American Distinguished Flying Cross. They were the first of many such awards in the Eighth.

The American crews would undertake one further raid before, courtesy of the RAF, they procured their own Bostons and returned to Molesworth. Here they were temporarily stood down whilst they prepared their new aircraft for action, including the application of the soon-to-be-familiar white star insignia of the U.S. Army Air Force.

HEROICS AT DE KOOY | Richard Taylor

Captain Charles C. Kegelman battles to keep his all-American crewed Boston in the air after it was hit by ground fire during the raid on De Kooy airfield, 4 July 1942.

Carrying General Ira C. Eaker, Commanding Officer of VIII Bomber Command, B-17E 'Yankee Doodle'
runs up her engines prior to the 'Mighty Eighth's' first official mission of the war, 17 Aug 1942.

THE FIRST 'OFFICIAL' MISSION

TUESDAY 17 AUGUST 42
VIII BOMBER COMMAND MISSION #1
97th BG, 17.40 hrs ROUEN France

By the middle of August 1942 the Eighth was no longer wholly reliant on aircraft 'borrowed' from the RAF. Weeks of easterly transhipments of both aircraft and their flight crews across the Atlantic meant that there were now three Bomb Groups either in England, or in the process of arriving. The 301st BG was equipped, fully manned and well into pre-combat training and the 92nd BG was transiting fast. However, it was the 97th BG that was first out of the blocks and ready to conduct combat missions using their own machines, albeit with fighter cover provided by the RAF.

At 15.12 hrs on Tuesday 17 August, after weeks of intensive training and setbacks caused by the vagaries of the English weather, six B-17E Flying Fortresses from the 97th BG took off from Polebrook to liaise with a large force of Spitfires. Splitting into two flights, their task was to act as a diversionary feint across the Channel, drawing the Luftwaffe fighters away from the main action of the day, the Eighth's first 'official' mission – a raid by another 12 Flying Fortresses from the 97th BG departing 15 minutes later from nearby Grafton Underwood to attack the extensive railway marshalling yards at Rouen.

Consisting of two flights of six aircraft, the main formation headed for northern France with B-17 *Butcher Shop* leading the first flight and carrying the 97th Group Commander, Colonel Frank Armstrong in the co-pilot's seat. Piloting the aircraft was Major Paul W. Tibbets who would later fly the B-29 Superfortress *Enola Gay* on the 6 August 1945 mission to drop the first atomic bomb on Hiroshima. Leading the second flight was B-17 *Yankee Doodle* carrying the Commanding Officer of VIII Bomber Command, Brigadier General Ira Eaker, who, in order to fly alongside some of the men under his command, had chosen to take part personally in the mission.

Despite some minor flak damage to a couple of machines, all aircraft returned safely.

What followed, however, was a different story because the main purpose behind the Eighth's 'Bomber Mission #1' was to help in softening up the enemy's transport infrastructure in support of a huge amphibious raid on Dieppe to be launched two days later.

WEDNESDAY 19 AUGUST 42
DIEPPE France

The strength of the Eighth Air Force was growing by the day. To support the growing number of bombers three Fighter Groups were already in the country and by mid-August a fourth was arriving. The fighters were under the control of Brigadier General Frank O'Driscoll 'Monk' Hunter at VIII Fighter Command headquarters at Bushey Hall near Watford, whose name had confusing similarities to the Eighth's overall headquarters at Bushy Park in Richmond.

In the month that had passed since the first Eighth fighter pilot had flown a mission over enemy territory – when in March Major Cecil P. Lessig flew a Spitfire with 64 Squadron RAF on a sweep over France – another pilot was claiming America's first victory of the war over a German aircraft. But it happened nowhere near England, or France for that matter, but in Iceland when, on 14 August, Lieutenant Elza K. Shahan flying a Lockheed P-38 Lightning with the First Fighter Group – 27th Fighter Squadron, finished off a long-range Focke-Wulf Fw200 Condor reconnaissance aircraft which had been sighted over the island.

In England it was the 31st Fighter Group that became the Eighth's first fighter group to be declared operational and their Spitfires were quickly, and proudly, adorned with U.S. roundels. With a few practice cross-channel sweeps alongside the RAF under their belts, on 19 August they claimed the Eighth's first air-to-air victory by a pilot flying from England when Second Lieutenant Samuel F. Junkin of the 309th Fighter Squadron shot down an Fw 190 in combat over Dieppe.

The Allied amphibious raid on Dieppe, however, was a bloody disaster. Despite the pounding of nearby Luftwaffe airfields, in which 22 of the Eighth's B-17s had participated, the skies over the battered French port saw ferocious air battles but nothing to compare with the carnage on the ground where more than 6,000 troops, spearheaded by a force of 5,000 Canadians, had been met by well-prepared, dug-in German forces on high alert.

The raid, too large for an effective 'hit-and-run' commando-style operation yet too small for a proper invasion, had been designed to test the ability of Allied troops to seize and hold a fortified French port. How they would extricate themselves was another matter because the planners had not only failed to identify the complex web of enemy guns concealed in the bluffs overlooking the beach, but gravely misjudged the gradient and composition of the beach. Most of the Canadians' tanks got stuck in the deep shingle to become sitting ducks for the German artillery. Few made it into town. On the beaches the now unsupported infantry landed in a blizzard of enemy fire. At 11.00am, faced with total annihilation, the order was given to withdraw. By the time the last survivor had been taken off, two-thirds of the Canadians were either dead, wounded or been taken prisoner.

The casualty figures might have been even worse had more enemy aircraft managed to get through the Allies' embattled fighter screen, and here too the losses were high – over 100 aircraft were lost, including eight Spitfires and five pilots from the 31st.

FIRST OF MANY | Richard Taylor

Spitfires from the 31st Fighter Group in action over Dieppe on 19 August 1942. During the encounter Second Lieutenant Samuel F. Junkin from the 309th Fighter Squadron downed an Fw 190 to claim the Eighth's first air victory by a pilot flying from England.

EAGLE FORCE | Robert Taylor

THE EAGLES & THE EIGHTH

The 31st Fighter Group weren't the only Americans flying Spitfires over Dieppe that day; among the RAF squadrons providing fighter cover for the raid were the three 'American Eagle' squadrons – 71 Squadron, 121 Squadron and 133 Squadron.

The USAAF might have flown their first missions and suffered their first casualties of the European war but they were not, by a long way, the first Americans to fight in the skies over occupied Europe. Almost from day one, and long before America officially entered the war after Pearl Harbor, a steady stream of volunteers had made their way to the UK to do their bit in the fight against Hitler and the Nazis. It was, however, illegal for them to do so because of the laws governed by the American 'Neutrality Act'.

The Unites States forbade its citizens from joining the armed forces of another country yet, nevertheless, hundreds of men headed north across the 49th parallel into Canada to enlist. For most this meant the RCAF, but others made their way across the North Atlantic and straight to the UK to join the RAF, many overstating both their age and experience.

Seven American pilots officially flew combat with the RAF during the Battle of Britain, one of whom was Pilot Officer William Meade Lindsey Fiske who, before the war, had been an Olympic gold medal bobsleigh racer in both the 1928 and 1932 Winter Olympics. He was also a famed racing driver. Believing in the cause of defending British freedom from the Nazis, he joined the RAF to fly Hawker Hurricanes with 610 Squadron at Tangmere. On 16 August 1940 during an encounter with a Junkers Ju87 Stuka, his aircraft was severely hit by return enemy fire. Instead of abandoning his stricken fighter, Fiske tried to

'The English have been damn good to me in good times so naturally I feel I ought to try and help out in bad if I can. There are absolutely no heroics in my motives, I'm probably twice as scared as the next man, but if anything happens to me I at least can feel I have done the right thing...'
Pilot Officer Billy Fiske

EAGLES PREY | Robert Taylor

coax it back to base, but it caught fire just before he came in for an emergency 'belly-up' landing. The Hurricane burst into flames and Fiske was badly burned in the ensuing inferno. Sadly he died of shock the following day in hospital, the first American airman to be killed in action with the RAF.

By September 1940 there were enough experienced American pilots for RAF Fighter Command to bring them together to form 71 'Eagle' Squadron at Church Fenton which became operational at the beginning of February 1941. Two more 'Eagle' squadrons – 121 and 133 Squadrons RAF – followed and all three were known and respected for their professionalism, skills and tough fighting capabilities. The legend of the 'American Eagles' had been born.

TUESDAY 29 SEPTEMBER 42
DEBDEN Essex

With the ever-increasing build-up of the Eighth Air Force in the UK it was perhaps inevitable that the three 'Eagle' squadrons, all with highly-experienced and battle-hardened fighter pilots, would be transferred away from the RAF and into the arms of the United States Army Air Force. There were, however, a few problems – such as pilot wings; none of the 'Eagles' had U.S. wings, or ranks; some 'Eagles' were non-commissioned Sergeant Pilots, unlike their American counterparts who were all commissioned officers.

In the end a fair and very British compromise was agreed: on transfer the Sergeant Pilots would receive an immediate commission, officers would receive a promotion and, having earned their RAF pilot wings the hard way, they were allowed to keep them on their new American uniforms, albeit smaller and on the opposite side to the U.S. pilot wings each was automatically granted.

The official transfer took place at a rain-sodden Debden airfield on Tuesday 29 September. As the band played and 'Old Glory' ran up the flagpole, Major General Carl Spaatz, Commander of the Eighth, took the salute alongside Air Chief Marshal Sir Sholto Douglas, Commander-in-Chief of RAF Fighter Command. Under their new commander, Colonel Edward Anderson, the Fourth Fighter Group – still known as the 'Eagles' – was born and ready for action.

AMERICAN EAGLE | Richard Taylor

The Spitfire Mk V of Captain Don Gentile, 336 Fighter Squadron, Fourth Fighter Group – the Eagles, formed from the three RAF Eagle Squadrons on 12 September 1942.

OFF TO THE TWELFTH

SUNDAY 08 NOVEMBER 42
CASABLANCA Morocco

The Allied invasion of North Africa began with dawn landings in Vichy French Morocco, followed by two further landings in Algeria. Codenamed *Operation Torch*, the invasion forces took two days to overcome the resistance provided by Vichy French units. On 10 November the Allied Commander, Lt General Dwight D. Eisenhower, brokered a deal with French Admiral François Darlan, who immediately ordered all Vichy French forces to cease their opposition. The Allies had their foothold in North Africa.

To support them a new American air force had been established – the Twelfth, the backbone of which had, by and large, been trained by, or was part of, the Eighth. Among them were two Bomb Groups (H), the 301st BG, and the experienced 97th BG that had flown the Eighth's first 'official' mission from England. The Bostons of the 15th Bomb Squadron also transferred to the Twelfth, along with five Fighter Groups, leaving the 4th as the Eighth's only operational Fighter Group.

TUESDAY 01 DECEMBER 42
8thAF HQ, BUSHY PARK Richmond

As well as men and machines the Eighth also lost their Commander to the air operations in North Africa when Major General Carl Spaatz was appointed Air Advisor to General Eisenhower. For the moment the strength of the Eighth had been badly diminished and its great mission of strategic bombing now lay with just four Fortress-equipped Bomb Groups. Spaatz's successor as overall commander of the Eighth, Brigadier General Ira C. Eaker, could only describe it as "a piddling little force".

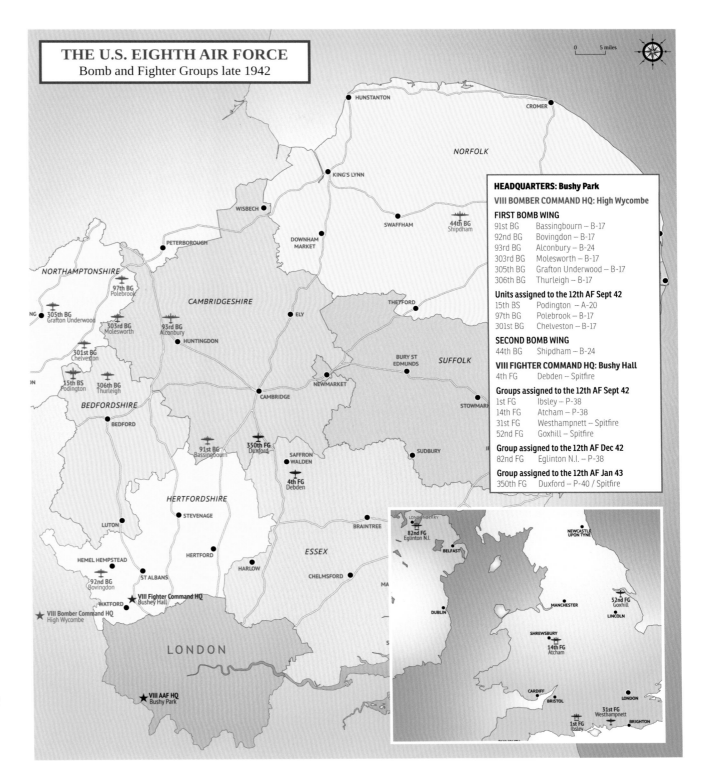

THE U.S. EIGHTH AIR FORCE
Bomb and Fighter Groups late 1942

0   5 miles

HEADQUARTERS: Bushy Park

VIII BOMBER COMMAND HQ: High Wycombe

FIRST BOMB WING
91st BG	Bassingbourn	– B-17
92nd BG	Bovingdon	– B-17
93rd BG	Alconbury	– B-24
303rd BG	Molesworth	– B-17
305th BG	Grafton Underwood	– B-17
306th BG	Thurleigh	– B-17

Units assigned to the 12th AF Sept 42
15th BS	Podington	– A-20
97th BG	Polebrook	– B-17
301st BG	Chelveston	– B-17

SECOND BOMB WING
44th BG	Shipdham	– B-24

VIII FIGHTER COMMAND HQ: Bushy Hall
4th FG	Debden	– Spitfire

Groups assigned to the 12th AF Sept 42
1st FG	Ibsley	– P-38
14th FG	Atcham	– P-38
31st FG	Westhampnett	– Spitfire
52nd FG	Goxhill	– Spitfire

Group assigned to the 12th AF Dec 42
82nd FG	Eglinton N.I.	– P-38

Group assigned to the 12th AF Jan 43
350th FG	Duxford	– P-40 / Spitfire

THE WOLFPACK | Robert Taylor

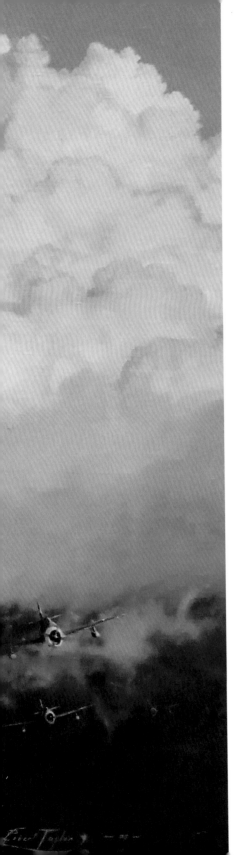

PART TWO: 1943

LIEUTENANT GENERAL IRA C. EAKER
COMMANDER OF THE EIGHTH AIR FORCE

1 December 1942 – 5 January 1944

Richard Taylor

Richard Taylor

POINTBLANK

THURSDAY 14 JANUARY 43
CASABLANCA Morocco

It was here, amidst the swaying palms and sun-swept villas of Morocco's largest city, that British Prime Minister Winston Churchill welcomed the arrival of U.S. President Franklin D. Roosevelt. Fresh from the success of *Operation Torch*, the Allied invasion of North Africa, two months earlier, the two leaders were here to discuss the progress of the war and, over the next ten days their respective Chief of Staffs and Joint Planners

successfully concluded a common strategy for the future, including the setting up of *Operation Pointblank* – a concentrated, combined bomber offensive by Britain and the United States against Germany designed to attack six main targets: U-boat construction yards and U-boat bases; the enemy aircraft industry – including the degradation of the Luftwaffe, both in the air and on the ground; transportation, oil production, both refineries and

storage facilities and, finally, factories manufacturing war matériel.

And, importantly, it was confirmed that the Americans would continue with their campaign of bombing by day, whilst the British bombed by night.

Through bitter experience and heavy losses, Bomber Command had all but forsaken daylight bombing in favour of night operations, but the Americans thought otherwise. Ever since their arrival in England almost a year before they continued to hone their skills using B-17 Flying Fortresses in daylight raids. But, as an exasperated Churchill stressed "…in the whole of the last six months of 1942 nothing had come of this immense effort – not a single bomb had been dropped on Germany".

That he now accepted the Eighth's daylight bombing role was largely down to the tact and diplomacy of its new Commander, General Ira Eaker. Churchill later wrote: "Eaker, however, pleaded his cause with skill and tenacity. He said it was quite true that they had not yet struck their blow – give them a month or two more and they would come into action on an ever-increasing scale. Considering how much had been staked on this venture by the United States and all they felt about it, I decided to back Eaker and his theme. I turned round completely and withdrew my opposition to the daylight bombing…"

It was settled. General Eaker now had the go-ahead he wanted and, thanks to Churchill's new-found support, Washington would now give him the wherewithal to continue and enlarge the whole doctrine of daylight precision bombing as a basic element of Allied air strategy. Eaker reckoned he would need a force of at least 800 B-17s and B-24s to implement the Eighth's contribution to *Operation Pointblank*. In addition to his bomber force, Eaker also knew he had to amass and build reliable fighter protection, meaning hundreds more single engine fighters had to be produced and delivered to the United Kingdom. But to attain such numbers would take several months.

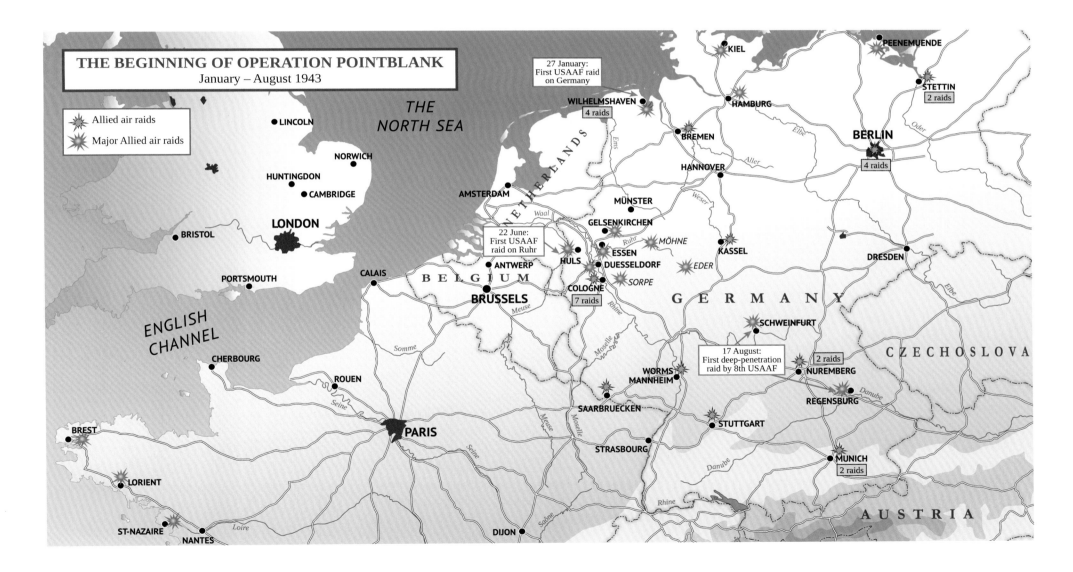

THE BEGINNING OF OPERATION POINTBLANK
January – August 1943

27 January:
First USAAF raid
on Germany

Allied air raids

Major Allied air raids

THE NORTH SEA

KIEL

PEENEMUENDE

STETTIN
2 raids

LINCOLN

WILHELMSHAVEN
4 raids

HAMBURG

BERLIN
4 raids

NORWICH

BREMEN

HUNTINGDON

CAMBRIDGE

AMSTERDAM

HANNOVER

MÜNSTER

GELSENKIRCHEN

LONDON

22 June:
First USAAF
raid on Ruhr

MÖHNE

KASSEL

DRESDEN

BRISTOL

ESSEN

DUESSELDORF

EDER

HULS

PORTSMOUTH

CALAIS

ANTWERP

SORPE

COLOGNE
7 raids

BELGIUM

BRUSSELS

GERMANY

ENGLISH CHANNEL

SCHWEINFURT

CHERBOURG

2 raids

NUREMBERG

ROUEN

17 August:
First deep-penetration
raid by 8th USAAF

CZECHOSLOVA

WORMS
MANNHEIM

REGENSBURG

BREST

SAARBRUECKEN

STUTTGART

PARIS

STRASBOURG

MUNICH
2 raids

LORIENT

AUSTRIA

ST-NAZAIRE

NANTES

DIJON

Robert Taylor

TOUR OF DUTY
TWENTY-FIVE MISSIONS

WEDNESDAY 19 MAY 43
BASSINGBOURN Cambridgeshire

At the beginning, flying combat missions in the Eighth Air Force had been harder than the bomber crews ever imagined. It wasn't just the physical fatigue of those long, bitterly cold hours spent in the air, often under fire; it was the morale-sapping thought that your odds of survival were bleak. Loss rates on the Eighth's early missions were high, it wasn't 'if' you were shot down but 'when'; and when that happened you'd probably be killed, or wounded, or at best, taken prisoner.

With two years of combat experience to draw on, those in charge of RAF Bomber Command had quickly realised that if their airmen were going to operate to the best of their abilities, then they'd need a break, time to rest, recover and hopefully a

chance to pass on some of their hard-won knowledge to others. Through trial, and a lot of error, Bomber Command had set the number of missions that any airman should complete before taking a rest at thirty.

Flying its daylight operations, the leaders of Eighth Air Force Bomber Command decided on 25 combat missions to complete a full tour, but with losses running as high as they were, even that figure seemed unobtainable. But there was soon light at the end of the tunnel: the ever-increasing range of their fighter protection.

Although it would be months before North American's P-51 Mustangs came into full operational service with the ability to escort their charges to any target in Germany, the Eighth's Lockheed P-38 Lightnings and Republic P-47 Thunderbolts were at least getting external fuel tanks which

RETURN OF THE BELLE | Robert Taylor

SOME OF THE CREW | Richard Taylor

Eight of 'Memphis Belle's' ten crew after the completion of its 25th mission (l to r): T/Sgt Robert Hanson (Radio Operator), Capt James Verinis (Co-Pilot), Capt Robert Morgan (Pilot), Capt Charles Leighton (Navigator), S/Sgt John Quinlan (Tail Gunner), S/Sgt Casimer Nastal (Waist Gunner), Capt Vincent Evans (Bombardier), and S/Sgt Clarence Winchell (Waist Gunner).

greatly increased their range. However, they still couldn't fly all the way with the bombers to the deepest penetration targets, but it was better than nothing. As a result of the extending range of fighter protection loss rates started to improve, and with it the chance of actually completing those 25 missions.

The famed *Memphis Belle* wasn't the first 'heavy' in the Eighth Air Force to reach the target; that honour fell to *Hot Stuff*, a Consolidated B-24 Liberator with the 93rd Bomb Group who completed her 25th mission on 7 February 1943. And the *Memphis Belle* wasn't the first Fortress either; *Delta Rebel No. 2*, a B-17F flying out of Bassingbourn with the 91st BG, claimed that distinction on 1 May. But the *Belle* was the most famous – thanks to the influence and glamour of a well-oiled public relations machine.

Touching down at Bassingbourn on 19 May, eighteen days after *Delta Rebel No. 2*, the *Belle* had the honour of being the second B-17 in the 91st Bomb Group to complete her 25 missions, ironically two days after her usual pilot, Captain Robert K. Morgan and most of her crew had done the same since they, like many crews, occasionally flew other aircraft. And now Captain Morgan and his crew were ordered to bring the *Memphis Belle* home to America for her next mission: a high-profile, morale-boosting, 31-city publicity and War-Bond selling tour. The following year, the crew of the *Memphis Belle* would feature in a movie directed and produced by the acclaimed Hollywood film director, William Wyler.

After completing 48 missions *Hell's Angels* went home for her own tour of fame, but for *Hot Stuff* the story ends with tragedy. On 3 May 1943, the day she and

her crew were due to fly back to the States, Lieutenant General Frank M. Andrews, Commander of the European Theatre of Operations, and several of his staff who'd been ordered back to Washington, took the places of five of the B-24's regular crew. It was a fateful choice. Crossing over south-east Iceland, *Hot Stuff* ran into bad weather and, in zero visibility, crashed into a mountain killing all on board except Sergeant George Eisel, the tail gunner.

In the spring of 1943, concentrated attacks by increasingly large formations of enemy fighters were taking their toll, not just the number of aircraft shot down but, by striking just as the bomber stream was making its bomb run, accuracy was being badly disrupted.

There were now three Eighth Air Force Fighter Groups fully operational. Joining the 4th Fighter Group were the 56th and the 78th Fighter Groups, all equipped with the rugged Republic P-47 Thunderbolt. But even with extended long-range drop tanks, the deepest penetration missions were still beyond their reach. For a while it was believed that special, heavily-armed and armoured B-17 YB-40 '*Gunships*' might provide the formations with greater defensive firepower, but they proved to be far too slow and unable to keep up with the normal speed of the bomber stream. It would be a while before the bombers could be protected by a capable fighter with the necessary range. That would eventually come with the introduction of the North American P-51 Mustang, but that was months away and for now the bomber crews would have to fight the Luftwaffe as best they could. The cost, however, would be high.

HOT STUFF | Richard Taylor

On 7 February 1943, 'Hot Stuff', a B-24D flying with the 330th BS, 93rd BG, became the first heavy bomber in the Eighth Air Force to complete 25 missions.

PLOESTI – THE VITAL MISSION | Robert Taylor

THE TRIP TO HELL AND BACK

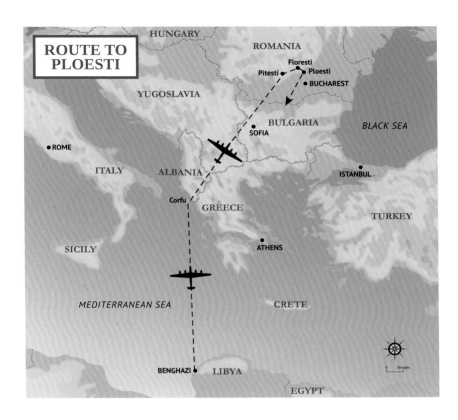

ROUTE TO PLOESTI

SUNDAY 01 AUGUST 43
PLOESTI Romania

Oil – the lifeblood that drives the machines of war. Every truck, tank, armoured vehicle, aircraft and naval vessel in the German arsenal depended on it. Ever since Romania had allied herself to Hitler's Germany in 1941, her huge complex of oil fields and refineries at Ploesti, and nearby Campina, thirty miles north of Bucharest, now provided a large percentage of German petroleum needs. Churchill called Ploesti, 'the taproot of German might'.

Much of the oil supplying the German armies on the Eastern Front and North Africa was transported directly from the Ploesti refineries. If those facilities could therefore be destroyed, or even badly damaged, Germany would be dealt a heavy blow from which it might never recover. Unsurprisingly the Germans transformed Ploesti into one of the most heavily-defended areas within the Third Reich.

The attack planned for August 1943, codenamed *Operation Tidal Wave*, wasn't the first time the Americans had visited Ploesti. In June the previous year Colonel Harry Halverson had attacked the area in a raid emulating the Doolittle attack on Tokyo. Instead of an aircraft carrier, Halverson had based his small force of B-24s on an RAF airfield in Egypt, and although the operation he led did manage to get through and hit the target, the damage was insignificant. The Germans, however, were quick to respond – by increasing the already heavy defences even more. It was obvious that the planned attack would be met with a savage response; it would require inspired leadership, precision flying, cool heads and, above all, courage – because the bomber force would be flying alone, without fighter escort.

Well beyond the range of any bomber based in England, overall responsibility for the mission therefore rested with the Ninth Air Force, operating from their airfields in Libya. The aircraft most suited to such a long-range operation – one involving a 2,000 mile round trip – was the Consolidated B-24D Liberator, but the Ninth only operated two B-24 Bomb Groups, the 98th BG and the 376th BG. To make a significant impact, a much larger force would be needed and so three further B-24 Bomb Groups involving 124 aircraft were temporarily assigned from the Eighth – the 44th BG and 93rd BG, and the 389th BG who had only just arrived in the UK.

The three Eighth Air Force B-24 Groups, having departed England to be welcomed by the unfriendly heat and dust of their temporary new homes on the North Africa coast, initially found themselves flying operations alongside the two B-24 Groups from the Ninth Air Force in support of *Operation Husky*, the Allied invasion of Sicily. Soon, however, both the Eighth and Ninth B-24 crews embarked on several weeks' exhaustive low-flying training exercises before being sent to their final base

SUZY Q | Richard Taylor

With 44th Bomb Group commander Colonel Leon Johnson directing operations from the Co-Pilot's seat, Major William Brandon steers B-24 'Suzy Q', lead ship of the 67th Bomb Squadron, through the maelstrom of smoke and fire engulfing the refineries at Ploesti, 1 August 1943.

near Benghazi, Libya. At first light on Sunday 1 August 1943, 178 heavily-laden B-24s lifted off from their desert runways for their 2,400 mile round trip to Ploesti.

Things went badly from the outset. Almost immediately the lead aircraft, engines clogged by sand, crashed. She was carrying the raid's lead navigator. Then, upon reaching the Albanian coast, and still under radio silence, they encountered thick cloud over the mountains which split up the formations, with some assuming the wrong course; German radar and Bulgarian fighters then spotted the leading group and any element of surprise was lost. By the time bomber force reached Ploesti the Germans were ready and waiting.

The planners had never expected an easy ride but, as the first B-24s made their run on to the target the intensity of the flak through which they flew was beyond belief; no one had experienced its like before. As the first bombs fell, the area erupted into a hell on earth, a morass of thick, dark oil-laden clouds billowing from burning facilities, the flight-path lit, not by daylight, but by sheets of flame and vivid flashes of bursting shells and exploding bombs, and, for those who survived the ordeal, the return home was little easier as enemy fighters pursued and harried the damaged departing bombers. Finally, after 16 hours in the air, running on fumes and with two engines out, the last of the survivors limped home and touched down. It was a miracle that anyone had got home at all.

Over 50 aircraft were lost and all but 35 had sustained serious damage. Over three hundred American airmen had been killed, and more than a hundred interned in neutral Turkey as prisoners of war. The heavy losses reinforced the countless acts of heroism that had taken place, a day on which more decorations for bravery were awarded than any other mission of the war. And, for those that took part, it came as no surprise that five Medals of Honor were awarded – two posthumously – the highest number ever granted for a single military action in American history. Four of those went to members of the Eighth.

Despite all the heroism and sacrifice it didn't take long for the Germans to repair the damage the B-24s had inflicted. The use of slave labour soon saw the rebuilding of damaged refineries and repairs to burning wells; within a few weeks most of Ploesti's oil facilities were back to full production and once again their precious oil was flowing to the front.

The Americans, however, would re-visit Ploesti refineries several times, mainly as a target for the 15th Air Force. These ensuing raids, carried out from high altitude, would prove far more successful due to better fighter protection – the introduction of the new long-range North American P-51 Mustang.

Colonel Leon Johnson, CO of the 44th Bomb Group, was one of four Eighth Air Force airmen to be awarded the Medal of Honor for the August 1943 Ploesti mission.

The citation for his award concludes with the words: "Col. Johnson's personal contribution to the success of this historic raid, and the conspicuous gallantry in action, and intrepidity at the risk of his life above and beyond the call of duty demonstrated by him on this occasion constitute such deeds of valor and distinguished service as have during our Nation's history formed the finest traditions of our Armed Forces."

INTO THE FIRE | Anthony Saunders

Facing the full effects and heavy smoke of the raging oil fires below, B-24 'Fertile Myrtle' and Liberators of the 98th Bomb Group, Ninth Air Force, pass over the Astra Romana refinery at Ploesti, 1 August 1943.

RETURN FROM SCHWEINFURT | Robert Taylor

REGENSBURG & SCHWEINFURT:
NAMES THEY WOULD COME TO DREAD

TUESDAY 17 AUGUST 43
`SCHWEINFURT Germany`

It was exactly a year since the Eighth Air Force had carried out its first 'official' mission of the war. Then, on 17 August 1942, a small group of B-17E Fortresses had attacked the Sotteville marshalling yards in Rouen. Now a hugely superior force, numbering 377 B-17s, was about to embark on the Eighth's most ambitious undertaking to date – a complex two-pronged 'double-strike' deep into the heart of Bavaria. And, like the raid on Ploesti a few weeks earlier, much of it would be far beyond the range of any fighter escort. They, too, would be alone.

The first of the strikes would see Colonel Curtis LeMay lead 147 B-17s from the Eighth's Third Air Division across the width of Germany to bomb the large Messerschmitt factory complex at Regensburg, a plant turning out over 300 Bf 109 fighter aircraft every month. In an effort to confuse the enemy and minimize their exposure to enemy fighters, the plan called for the Regensburg-bound B-17s (fitted with long-range rubberised 'Tokyo' tanks) to then fly on to airfields in North Africa rather than return to England, a lengthy trip of covering some 1,500 miles. It was hoped the German fighters would be left prowling empty skies waiting for bombers that wouldn't re-appear.

The second strike called for an even larger force; some 230 Fortresses from the First Air Division, led by Brigadier General Robert B. Williams, were to head for the anti-friction ball-bearing factories at Schweinfurt. It was expected that the Regensburg force in the lead would encounter the stiffest opposition from enemy fighters on the route across Germany and, with careful timing, the Schweinfurt force, following, would find the enemy

getting low on fuel and ammunition and hopefully be forced to land and replenish. The long journey home, however, would probably be a very different story.

Would it all work? The complexity and timings of this double plan were a colossal undertaking: they would be going deeper into Germany than ever before, much of it without fighter protection. And once the Germans had figured out what was going on, the crews knew that at some point they were in for a very rough ride – probably the roughest they, or anybody else, had seen before. It was clear that some of them wouldn't be coming home.

As in all wars even the best-laid plans can go wrong – and this Tuesday they did, almost immediately, when thicker than expected mist and swirling fog delayed

take-off and raised tensions even higher. To make it to North Africa in daylight, LeMay's formations needed every hour of daylight they could possibly get. He had, however, methodically trained his Wing in instrument take-offs, ready for just such an occasion as this. With the help of the ground crew holding torches to light the taxiways, he eventually got his Regensburg force airborne, albeit 90 minutes late.

The Schweinfurt group, however, was delayed far longer. So long that the escort fighters that had covered LeMay's Regensburg force across Belgium had the opportunity of returning to England, land, re-fuel and re-arm, and get airborne again. Ominously the Luftwaffe had time in hand to do the same. When the Schweinfurt-

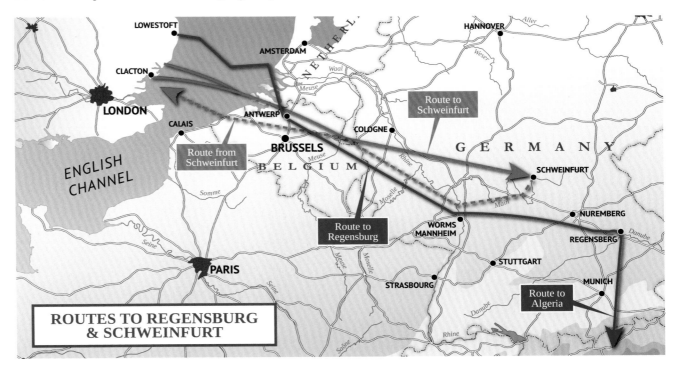

ROUTES TO REGENSBURG & SCHWEINFURT

bound crews finally got airborne and in formation, they were almost four hours behind schedule and the enemy was ready and waiting. The bomber crews had been briefed for a hard journey home; now it looked as if they were going to be hammered in both directions.

Having crossed the Belgian coast their fighter escort, even with recently added drop tanks, ran out of range and, for the second time that morning, were forced to break off and return to their bases in England. For the next few hours both unescorted groups would now have to run the gauntlet on their own.

As the Luftwaffe pounced, the on-going battle became the most terrifying ordeal that many had ever faced as the close-packed bombers crossed over Germany at a stately 180 mph; their progress charted by a trail of flame, smoke, explosions, parachutes, men and debris

from damaged or disintegrating aircraft. Of the bombers in the Regensburg force, 24 Fortresses were lost and more than 50 had been damaged, 200 men were missing in action whilst another nine returned home badly wounded along with the bodies of four dead. But, if there was to be consolation, the raid was deemed a success: a large part of the Messerschmitt plant was left smouldering in ruins and the assembly of Bf 109 fighters was disrupted for months.

The Schweinfurt force was hit even harder, 36 aircraft lost and 121 damaged, three beyond repair, and casualties were inevitably higher too: 352 men missing in action and of the returnees 12 airmen were badly wounded, with several dead. Although serious damage had been inflicted on the ball-bearing factories the raid hadn't delivered the killer blow the Eighth Air Force

Bomber Command had hoped for. The only positive moment came when returning: 'Hub' Zemke and the P-47s of the 56th Fighter Group, tasked with protecting the returning bombers over Belgium, had got into position earlier than the Germans expected and taking them by surprise, the fighter pilots of the 56th FG quickly destroyed 17 Luftwaffe fighters and, much to the relief of the bomber crews, finally drove the enemy away.

THE WOLFPACK STRIKES | Richard Taylor

P-47s from the 63rd FS, 56th FG dive at speed to strike at the German fighters attacking the lead formations of B-17s returning from Schweinfurt, 17 August 1943.

BLACK THURSDAY
IT'S SCHWEINFURT – AGAIN

THURSDAY 14 OCTOBER 43

SCHWEINFURT Germany

England was experiencing its mildest October since 1921, but the ridge of low pressure that was slowly tracking east over Iceland had brought damp, dull and overcast skies to East Anglia. A month had passed since the Eighth's four Bomb Wings had been re-formed into three new Bomb Divisions – the First, commanded by Major General Robert B. Williams who'd led the 17 August mission to Schweinfurt, the Second under Major General James P. Hodges whose son of the same name served as a fighter pilot in the 56th Fighter Group, whilst Curtis LeMay, newly promoted Brigadier General, took charge of the Third.

The Eighth Air Force was currently facing its toughest challenge to date; aircraft losses were higher than ever but, more importantly, so too were the increasing number of young airmen lost in combat. In a seven day period commencing Friday 8 October 1943, in what would come to be known as 'Black Week', the Eighth Air Force would lose over 140 heavy bombers, 88 of them in just three days. Such was the desperate need for replacement aircraft and crews that, coupled with a spell of bad weather, the Eighth Air Force was stood down for three days to recover. On Thursday 14 October they were flying again, but today would prove more costly than ever.

Determined to keep the hard-won pressure up, General Eaker and Eighth Air Force Bomber Command decided this was the day to return to the primary target that hadn't been completely destroyed on that hellish mission in August – the ball-bearing factories of Schweinfurt!

On that Thursday morning the dreary overcast conditions that enveloped the 92nd Bomb Group's Fortresses on their hardstandings were no different to those at a host of other airfields across eastern England and, as the crews assembled in their briefing rooms at 05.00 hrs, the gloom outside was soon reflected in the mood of the men inside as the name of day's target was revealed – "It's Schweinfurt – again".

The shock was palpable. This was news that neither they, nor any of the 18 other Bomb Groups involved, wanted to hear. Despite the damage wreaked on the 17 August mission, the ball-bearing plant at Schweinfurt was still operating, but this time it was planned to send a mixed force of well over 400 B-17 Flying Fortresses and B-24 Liberators on the 960-mile, seven-hour round trip, to complete the job. For the second time in three months, the crews knew that the last 370 miles to the target were beyond the range of their fighter escorts; as soon as the escorts turned for home, the Luftwaffe were once again bound to pounce. Having faced the ordeal once before, it was a terrifying prospect.

The bad weather that had plagued the start of the 17 August mission was little better on that October morning; with visibility down to a quarter of a mile in places there were more than a few who hoped, if not prayed, that the mission might be cancelled. But they were to be disappointed; the weather over mainland Europe was reported to be clearing and the skies over the target were expected to be crisp and unobstructed.

Shortly before 10.00 hrs the order was given to start engines – the raid was on. But not in the strength intended. The foul, foggy weather over Norfolk meant that only 29 of the planned force of 60 B-24s managed to get airborne, and of these, eight got lost in heavy cloud. The 21 that remained now constituted a force far too small for the difficult mission ahead and, instead of

Robert Taylor

continuing to Schweinfurt, they were dispatched to a secondary diversionary target, hoping to divert at least some of enemy fighters from the main striking force.

The 149 B-17s of the First Division, with mission commander Colonel 'Budd' J. Peaslee flying alongside Captain James K. McLaughlin of the 92nd BG, did manage to assemble successfully, and they headed out over the North Sea, across the Netherlands to the German border, setting a straight course to Schweinfurt. As expected the moment their escorts departed, the Luftwaffe struck and as with the August raid, the relentless assault lasted all the way to the target. With enemy fighters spewing a continuing barrage of cannon-fire and rockets into the American formations, losses grew as the miles ticked slowly by. By the time they reached Schweinfurt less than half of the First Division remained airborne but, undeterred by the mayhem around them, the survivors held their course and bombed successfully. All the targets were hit; now all they had to do was fight their way back.

The Third Division, following on a slightly more southerly route, had fared better on the journey to Schweinfurt but the accuracy of their bombing was hindered by the targets being partially obscured by smoke from the First Division's attack. Now as the Third Division turned for home, it was their turn to take a pummelling, and worse was to come. The murk that had hindered the B-24 force earlier in the day had closed in, keeping the hoped-for escorts grounded. As the Third Division neared the Channel coast it wasn't friendly fighters they met, but Luftwaffe Focke-Wulf Fw 190s – and they were anything but friendly.

Bruised, battered and running out of fuel, the survivors staggered home, with some just glad to put down on the nearest airfield they could find. Although the raid had destroyed production – it would be months before the ball-bearing plants were running smoothly again – the overall losses suffered by the Eighth were again horrendous. Although deemed a strategic success, if the Eighth continued to take losses on this scale it wouldn't be long before it ceased to exist as an effective fighting force and the doctrine of its daylight strategic bombing campaign was now in serious jeopardy. The losses simply could not be sustained; the average life expectancy of an Eighth Air Force bomber crew was now just seven missions, a far cry from the required 25 missions to complete a tour. With an average age span between 19 and 22 years old, the odds stacked against the young airmen were proving difficult to live with.

On that 'bloody Thursday' the Luftwaffe hadn't had things all their own way; undeterred by the losses, the Fortress gunners had shot down and destroyed 186 enemy fighters – and those, unlike the American bombers, would be hard to replace.

Tactics and strategies had to change immediately or the future of the Eighth Air Force would be a dim reality. Salvation, however, was on hand. Just four weeks after the raid the first long-range P-51 Mustangs were ready for combat, albeit supplied by the Ninth Air Force. The Fortresses would no longer be alone.

SCHWEINFURT – THE SECOND MISSION | Robert Taylor

A PACK OF WOLVES | Robert Taylor

THE WOLFPACK STIRS
'HUB' ZEMKE & THE 56th FIGHTER GROUP

Richard Taylor

SATURDAY 30 OCTOBER 43
HALESWORTH Suffolk

When Major 'Hub' Zemke took command of the newly-formed 56th Fighter Group, one of the first things that concerned him was the performance of the P-47 Thunderbolts with which they'd been equipped. The 56th were the first group in the Eighth to receive Republic's new fighter and it was huge, a massive beast of an aircraft. Weighing in at nearly 12,000lbs on take-off, it was a far cry from the nimble Spitfires that the Fourth Fighter Group was flying, and twice as heavy. It certainly lived up to its nickname – the 'Jug'.

Zemke was neither impressed with its lack of power on climbing, nor its manoeuvrability at low level. But, at altitude, when the exhaust gas-driven turbo-supercharger took hold, he loved it. Above 17,500 feet, the 'Jug' became a thoroughbred.

So, whilst other groups re-equipping with P-47s moaned, especially the Fourth, Zemke persevered and came up with a tactic to get the best out of these massive machines – he'd climb. Reckoning that the bomber streams usually flew at altitudes between 20,000 and 24,000 feet, he'd seen the Luftwaffe fighters climb to engage them. What if his P-47s were already high above the bombers? Zemke took his P-47s up much higher, between 25,000 and 27,000 feet, and used the Thunderbolts' extraordinary diving speed to full advantage. He now not only had surprise on his side but unmatchable speed.

"The added 2,000 feet," he said, "gave us the advantage of a good attacking dive speed"… Recognising the Thunderbolts' qualities, the Wolfpack's tactics soon evolved into a series of dive-and-zoom manoeuvers. With the emphasis on keeping the Jug's flying speed

Richard Taylor

44

up and with much training, the tactic soon involved an entire flight, and ultimately a complete squadron, in the attack. Zemke was a brilliant tactician and skilled leader. His use of the Thunderbolts' attributes of speed and dive characteristics were honed into the development of the 'Zemke fan', which used the fire power of a flight of fighters to box in the enemy aircraft and trap them into an almost impossible escape. The word of the day was 'If you can't take the target out on the first pass, set up the situation for the following flight or squadron to make their kill.' It became a team effort."

By the end of August 1943 the 56th were the leading Fighter Group in the Eighth and, on 4 October, Zemke notched up his own fifth victory – he too was now an Ace.

On Saturday 30 October 1943 Colonel Zemke was ordered to rest and finally relinquished command of the 56th Fighter Group. But it wasn't for long; in January 1944 he returned for a second tour, once again in command of the 56th. Under Zemke's leadership – he was once described as 'the greatest fighter leader of the war', the 56th FG scored over 500 air victories, three-quarters of their eventual tally, destroying more enemy aircraft in combat than any other group in the Eighth.

Zemke, however, wasn't in command of the 56th to witness the end of hostilities. In August 1944 he was transferred to command the 479th Fighter Group flying newly acquired P-51 Mustangs. The newest and least experienced fighter group, the 479th had just lost their commander, Lieutenant Colonel Kyle Riddle, in a strafing attack. But Zemke's new posting didn't last long. On 30 October the wing of his P-51 was ripped off in a violent bout of sudden turbulence. Forced to bail out over enemy territory, he was captured and taken prisoner, spending the rest of the war as Senior PoW Officer at Stalag Luft I in Germany. Having flown the last of his 154 combat missions, for Zemke the war was over, unlike his predecessor. Somehow, with the help of the French Resistance, Colonel Riddle had managed to evade capture and returned to England to resume his old command.

Colonel Francis S. 'Gabby' Gabreski

The top-scoring American Ace in Europe

Robert Taylor

The son of Polish immigrants, 'Gabby' Gabreski had been one of the few American pilots to get airborne during the infamous Japanese raid on Pearl Harbor on 7 December 1941 but, with his knowledge and love of all things Polish, he transferred to England, serving with 315 Polish Squadron RAF flying Spitfire Mk.IXs. Transferring to 'Hub' Zemke's 56th Fighter Group, he notched up an unbeatable tally in the ETO of 28 air victories, plus another three destroyed on the ground.

'Wait till you get 'em in the sights,' he used to say, 'then short bursts. There's no use melting your guns!'

By 20 July 1944 he'd flown 300 combat hours and was scheduled for a rest. But he fancied just one final mission. It turned out to be his last. On the way home from escorting bombers he spotted a Heinkel He-111 parked on a German airfield and decided to strafe it on a low-level run, but he got too low. The propeller of Gabreski's Thunderbolt struck the ground and he was forced to crash-land. Eventually he was taken prisoner after five days on the run, he was sent to Stalag Luft I to be greeted in person by the camp's senior officer – none other than his former commander, Colonel 'Hub' Zemke.

ZEMKE'S WOLFPACK | Robert Taylor

High over Germany and at the extremity of their range, Hub Zemke and his 'Wolfpack' dive to defend a damaged B-17 from persistent attack by a group of marauding Fw 190s during the summer of 1944.

END OF YEAR

FRIDAY 24 DECEMBER 43
V-1 CONSTRUCTION SITES Pas-de-Calais

It might have been Christmas Eve but today the Eighth launched its largest number of bombers to date. With 26 Bomb Groups now operational, a total of 670 heavies were sent to attack nearly two dozen V-1 rocket sites under construction in the Pas-de-Calais and the first of many similar operations mounted by the Eighth during the latter portion of the war.

Fortunately, considering that Christmas Day was upon them, not a single aircraft was lost and the end of the month hailed as a milestone. During the month of December the Eighth had dropped 13,142 tons of bombs, the first time they'd exceeded that dropped by RAF Bomber Command.

The Eighth's fighters were experiencing a milestone too: numbers were expanding. Three days after Christmas the 20th Fighter Group and their P-38s became the Eighth's eleventh operational fighter group, and whilst none of the new Merlin-powered Mustangs had yet found their way to any of them, those of the Ninth's 354th Fighter Group had been placed under the Eighth's operational control, with former 133 Eagle Squadron pilot, Major Donald J. M. Blakeslee, now an Ace with the Fourth, sent along to train the new and inexperienced pilots and lead them on five missions.

VIII Fighter Command had now flown over 17,500 operational sorties and destroyed more than 200 enemy aircraft, but big changes were in hand for everyone. The structure and organisation of all the American Air Forces in Europe was about to be re-organised, and the coming New Year would see a new commander at the helm of the Eighth.

"Few men can equal General Eaker's great stature as an air pioneer – we owe him our gratitude for his contributions to the Air Force and the nation."

General Larry Welch, Former Air Force Chief of Staff, August 1987

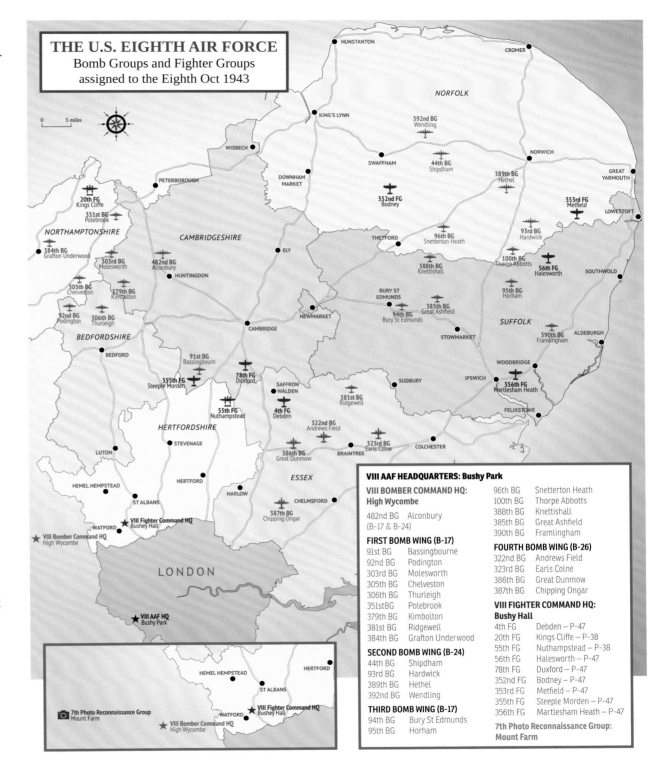

THE U.S. EIGHTH AIR FORCE
Bomb Groups and Fighter Groups
assigned to the Eighth Oct 1943

VIII AAF HEADQUARTERS: Bushy Park

VIII BOMBER COMMAND HQ: High Wycombe		
482nd BG Alconbury (B-17 & B-24)	96th BG	Snetterton Heath
	100th BG	Thorpe Abbotts
FIRST BOMB WING (B-17)	388th BG	Knettishall
91st BG Bassingbourne	385th BG	Great Ashfield
92nd BG Podington	390th BG	Framlingham
303rd BG Molesworth		
305th BG Chelveston	**FOURTH BOMB WING (B-26)**	
306th BG Thurleigh	322nd BG	Andrews Field
351st BG Polebrook	323rd BG	Earls Colne
379th BG Kimbolton	386th BG	Great Dunmow
381st BG Ridgewell	387th BG	Chipping Ongar
384th BG Grafton Underwood		

SECOND BOMB WING (B-24)

		VIII FIGHTER COMMAND HQ: Bushy Hall	
44th BG	Shipdham	4th FG	Debden – P-47
93rd BG	Hardwick	20th FG	Kings Cliffe – P-38
389th BG	Hethel	55th FG	Nuthampstead – P-38
392nd BG	Wendling	56th FG	Halesworth – P-47
		78th FG	Duxford – P-47
THIRD BOMB WING (B-17)		352nd FG	Bodney – P-47
94th BG	Bury St Edmunds	353rd FG	Metfield – P-47
95th BG	Horham	355th FG	Steeple Morden – P-47
		356th FG	Martlesham Heath – P-47

7th Photo Reconnaissance Group: Mount Farm

THE MIGHTY EIGHTH – COMING HOME | Robert Taylor

PART THREE: 1944

LIEUTENANT GENERAL JAMES H. DOOLITTLE
COMMANDER OF THE EIGHTH AIR FORCE

6 January 1944 – 9 May 1945

Richard Taylor

Richard Taylor

WIDEWING WIDENS

THURSDAY 06 JANUARY 44
8th AF HEADQUARTERS Bushy Park Richmond

With the reorganisation of the American Air Forces in Europe, and preparations for the forthcoming invasion across the Channel planned for the summer, the Eighth Air Force Headquarters at Bushy Park – codename *Widewing* – assumed a new mantle; it was now to become the headquarters of the newly-formed United States Strategic Air Forces in Europe – USSTAF, the command overseeing all strategic air operations against Germany. These included the Eighth Air Force in England alongside the Ninth Air Force, which had just completed operations in North Africa. The role of the Ninth would be to lend tactical support for the forthcoming invasion. Together with the Twelfth and Fifteenth Air Forces, who were stationed in the Mediterranean and Italy, the strategic

destruction of German military and infrastructure targets would now be re-evaluated and planned by Senior Allied Command.

The new commander of USSTAF was highly familiar with the surroundings at Bushy Hall because he was none other than the newly-promoted Lieutenant General Carl Spaatz, former commander of the Eighth.

Another General was moving in too – General Dwight D. Eisenhower, the Supreme Commander of the Allied Expeditionary Force, for Bushy Park was also to serve as his headquarters – Supreme Headquarters Allied Expeditionary Force, or SHAEF.

Whilst Spaatz settled in at Bushy Park in Richmond, General Eaker was given command of all Allied Air Forces in the Mediterranean Theatre. Eaker was replaced as Commander of the Eighth Air Force in January 1944

by legendary aviator and leader of the first retaliatory strike on Japan in April 1942, Lieutenant General James H. Doolittle, previously Commander of the Twelfth Air Force in North Africa. One of his first decisions was to return Eighth Air Force headquarters to High Wycombe, incorporating not only Eighth Air Force Bomber Command but Eighth Air Force Fighter Command as well.

The Eighth now had a new commander and under Doolittle's leadership things were about to radically change because, with the devastating losses incurred by the Eighth during the autumn, existing theories on conducting daylight strategic bombing was unsustainable. If the doctrine was to survive, new tactics and strategies were urgently needed.

MONDAY 31 JANUARY 44
LEISTON Suffolk
357th Fighter Group

The aircraft that the Eighth Air Force had been waiting so long for had so far failed to materialise. The North American P-51 Mustang, the fighter that almost everyone thought could solve many of the long-range escort problems, was still being primed for the Ninth Air Force. But following the reorganisation, and after much pressure, especially from Fourth Fighter Group Commander, Colonel Donald Blakeslee, priority was eventually switched to the Eighth.

But it wasn't Blakeslee's 'Eagles' who were the first beneficiaries; they had to wait a few more days for their Mustangs to arrive. The honour of being the Eighth's first P-51 Group fell to the Ninth Air Force's 357th Fighter Group through an unusual swap; on the last day of January the 357th flew from their temporary base at Raydon to their new home at Leiston to join the Eighth Air Force, whilst the 358th and their P-47s did the reverse journey to become part of the Ninth.

In the meantime, as plans progressed to transition the Eighth's other fighter groups on to the new Mustang, the existing P-38 and P-47 pilots still had a war to fight.

Doolittle was about to issue an order that involved a major change in the role of the fighters who, up until now, had been directed never to leave the bomber formations they were escorting. From now on they had leave to attack the Luftwaffe whenever, and wherever, they saw them. General Doolittle ordered his eager young fighter pilots to crush the Luftwaffe in any way possible. 'Your mission,' he declared, 'is to destroy the German Air Force.'

Robert Taylor

51

FIGHT FOR SUPREMACY

THURSDAY 10 FEBRUARY 44
HONINGTON Suffolk
364th Fighter Group

It was known that the P-38 Lightning packed a heavy punch with its nose-mounted 20mm cannon and four .50 machine guns, but by the beginning of 1944 they had largely been phased out in favour of the rugged and more reliable P-47 Thunderbolts, whilst the first P-51s were appearing in ever-increasing numbers. But operational duties for Lockheed's twin boom, twin engine fighter weren't over just yet. The 364th Fighter Group, which had only just arrived in England, were for the time being still equipped with Lightnings.

They arrived at Honington in Suffolk on 10 February 1944 but, like so many other Eighth Air Force units, they'd done their basic training in the warm sunny skies of Southern California. The transition to the vagaries of English winter weather took some adjusting but, nevertheless, they surprised observers by flying their first combat mission after just three weeks in the country. With the invasion looming they had a role to play so there was no period of grace.

As with the other Eighth Fighter Groups their primary task was still to provide cover for the B-17 and B-24 bomber formations, but with Doolittle's new instructions to attack as well as defend, it was hectic from day one. Theoretically their fighters were no match for the Luftwaffe's newer, more nimble Focke-Wulf Fw 190s in high altitude, one-on-one dogfights, but the rookie pilots of the 364th FG steadfastly managed to hold their own.

On D-Day and in the weeks immediately after the invasion, the 364th FG and their P-38s were to prove themselves invaluable tools, this time in support of the Allied armies on the ground as they strafed and dive-bombed convoys, railway yards, locomotives and trains, bridges, trucks and armoured vehicles and anything else that looked dangerous. It would be late July before the 364th said goodbye to their tired, battle-weary P-38s and exchanged them for gleaming new silver P-51Ds.

Robert Taylor

HOSTILE SKIES | Robert Taylor

Alone and falling behind the main formation, a damaged B-24 attracts the unwanted attention of two prowling Fw 190s. Luckily a pair of twin-boom P-38 Lightning escort fighters are on hand to deal with the situation.

BIG WEEK AND THE BIG 'B'

> 'When the will defies fear, when duty throws the gauntlet down to fate, when honor scorns to compromise with death – that is heroism.'
>
> Robert Green Ingersoll, 'The Great Agnostic'

VALOR AT POLEBROOK | Richard Taylor

Ball Turret Gunner Sgt. Archie Mathies and Navigator 2nd Lt. Walter Truemper from the 351st Bomb Group, make a third attempt to land their battle-damaged B-17 at Polebrook.

LEIPZIG Germany
305th Bomb Group

Increasingly the Eighth Air Force bomber offensive had been making its presence felt during the first two months of the year. Whilst the V-weapon sites along the coast continued to receive their share of attention, the targeting of German fighter production grew in intensity. Co-ordinating with RAF Bomber Command, their combined efforts to destroy the enemy's production of aircraft culminated in the last week of February 1944.

To the Eighth Air Force that period of operational intensity was officially deemed *Operation Argument* but to most, however, it would commonly be referred to as 'Big Week', a period in which Doolittle and Eighth Air

Force Bomber Command began an all-out push against selected strategic targets in Germany. On 20 February they put up over 1,000 heavies for the first time, their targets being a dozen different locations across the Reich.

It was also a day of unparalleled heroism, one on which no less than three Medals of Honor were awarded; two – to Sergeant Archie Mathies, a ball turret gunner, and Second Lieutenant Walter Truemper, the navigator of a 351st Group B-17 called *Ten Horsepower*, posthumously.

With their co-pilot dead, and pilot barely alive after a cannon shell had exploded in the cockpit, the crew

had been ordered to bale out, but Mathies and Truemper refused to abandon their gravely-wounded captain and valiantly attempted to bring their battered Fortress home. They almost made it, but the stricken bomber crashed on their third attempt to land at their base at Polebrook, disintegrating on landing. Mathies and Truemper were killed outright, and although the mortally wounded pilot survived the impact, he later died of his wounds.

WILLIAM LAWLEY – AGAINST ALL ODDS
Richard Taylor

Badly wounded and battling to remain conscious, pilot and Captain 1/Lt William Lawley from the 305th Bomb Group was awarded the Medal of Honor for bringing his wounded crew and crippled B-17 home to a successful crash-landing at RAF Redhill on 20 Feb 1944.

The third Medal of Honor awarded that day went to First Lieutenant William 'Bill' Lawley, pilot and Captain of a B-17 from the 364th Bomb Squadron, 305th Bomb Group. Assigned to attack a Messerschmitt assembly plant near Leipzig, the Lawley crew were unable to offload their bombs over the target due to severe icing in the release mechanism. They had just turned for home when disaster struck – a group of enemy fighters swept past in a savage head-on attack. The Fortress was struck several times, heavily damaging a wing

and setting one engine on fire. As Lawley pushed the stricken bomber into a steep dive to try and extinguish the fire in the burning engine, other shells exploded in the fuselage injuring the crew, some severely. Another 20mm shell burst through the front windscreen of the cockpit, instantly killing the co-pilot and lacerating 'Bill' Lawley's face, neck and hands.

In agony, his vision smeared by blood and with only one hand still functioning, Lawley battled to successfully bring his stricken aircraft under control. Believing the

Fortress might explode at any minute, he ordered the crew to bale out immediately. Lawley's flight engineer heeded the command but, as he did so, Lawley learned that two of his crew in the rear portion of the aircraft were so badly wounded that they were unable to strap on their parachutes.

Faced with a life or death dilemma of how to save their lives, Lawley opted to stay with the aircraft and try to get it home to England. The remaining crew, with complete confidence in Lawley, decided to stay with their pilot.

It was, however, the start of a five-hour nightmare as Luftwaffe fighters attacked the battered bomber once again as another engine began to burn but the badly wounded Lawley, in a display of extraordinary skill, managed to shake off his pursuers before collapsing through loss of blood. Coaxed back into consciousness by the bombardier, who was now manning the co-pilot's position, Lawley re-took control as they neared the English Channel. With one engine still burning and a second feathered, the crew managed to jettison their bombs into the waters below and, as they crossed the English coast, Lawley knew he had to put down, and fast.

The residents of Surrey were used to the sight of aircraft overhead, but were surprised to see a bomber coming in so low. Looking for a suitable field on which to land, Lawley spotted the inviting shape of RAF Redhill's grass strip and, taking a deep breath, brought his Fortress in for a successful crash-landing. Thanks to 'Bill' Lawley's heroism and brilliant airmanship all of the crew survived, even the flight engineer who'd baled out. He was captured and taken prisoner by the Germans.

In the seven days between the 19th and 25th February, the Eighth Air Force flew more than 3,300 sorties and dropped 6,000 tons of bombs, wreaking havoc on the industries directly, or indirectly, involved with German aircraft production. As output tumbled, the Luftwaffe was deprived of the replacements it now so badly needed because, during that week alone, over 500 German fighters had been shot down. The battle to destroy the Luftwaffe was slowly being won.

In this week of heroics the Eighth Air Force now had 30 Heavy Bomb Groups fully operational and, for the first time since their arrival almost two years ago, the Eighth surpassed RAF Bomber Command in numbers of both men and machines.

They now turned their attention to capital of the Third Reich, Berlin – the 'Big B'.

SATURDAY 04 MARCH 44
BERLIN Germany
95th & 100th Bomb Groups

RAF Bomber Command had first struck Berlin on 25 August 1940 during the Battle of Britain. A mixed force of 50 Wellingtons, Whitleys and Hampdens had bombed Hitler's capital in retaliation for bombs dropped on London the previous day. RAF Bomber Command had re-visited the city many times by night but a daylight attack on the city had never been attempted. Eighth Air Force Bomber Command, however, had been planning such a mission since the previous November, only to be thwarted in their plans by the crippling losses of aircraft and crewmen. Nevertheless, by March 1944, the Eighth Air Force had been rebuilt and was ready; the first daylight raid on the German capital was scheduled to take place on Friday 3 March.

The bomber crews were excited but apprehensive; everyone knew that Berlin was probably the most heavily defended target in the Third Reich and as one crewman noted 'we were all excited to go to Berlin, after all it was where Hitler lived. But we knew we were in for one hell of a fight'.

On the morning of 3 March the bomber force took off as planned. Assembled over East Anglia but heading east towards Germany they were confronted by a high wall of dense cumulus cloud. It would be impossible for the bomber stream to fly into such heavy cloud and maintain effective formation integrity. The mission was recalled.

The following day the Eighth Air Force once more selected Berlin as their primary target but again poor weather conditions, so often to interfere with the Eighth's operations, reigned supreme. As the heavies started assembling, thick cloud, biting winds and snow flurries forced the mission to be aborted and the bombers were recalled, but not everyone got the message.

Unaware of the recall, 31 Fortresses from two squadrons of the 95th BG, one from the 100th BG and a pathfinder from the 482nd BG pressed on towards Berlin with their P-51 fighter escorts from the 4th FG and 357th FG. The small American force successfully released their bombs on target, despite the presence of Luftwaffe fighters over the German capital. Although five aircraft were lost, the Eighth Air Force had inadvertently, but successfully, hit Berlin for the first time.

Two days later more than 700 heavies returned to hit Berlin, escorted by nearly 800 fighters. This time, however, a much larger force of Luftwaffe fighters was waiting and the savage encounter that followed proved to be one of the most costly air battles of the entire European campaign. Sixty-nine American heavy bombers and 14 fighters were lost.

But the Eighth would bounce back and with their fighter strength growing by the day, it was now the Luftwaffe who was losing control. Hermann Göring, head of the Luftwaffe, later told his American captors that the day he knew the war was lost was "When I saw your bombers over Berlin protected by your long-range fighters, I knew that the Luftwaffe would be unable to stop your bombers. Our weapons plants would be destroyed, our defeat was inevitable".

For once he was right. Having grown used to attack by night, now he and the rest of the Nazi-elite hunkered in Berlin would equally have no respite by day.

THE BLOODY HUNDREDTH | Richard Taylor

B-17s from the 100th Bomb Group.

Captain Don Gentile of the 336th Fighter Squadron and one of the Fourth Fighter Group's leading Aces with his P-51B (43-6913) 'Shangri-La' VF-T at Debden, March 1944.

THE BUILD-UP TO OVERLORD

SUNDAY 05 MARCH 44
WESTERN FRANCE
4th Fighter Group

There was little doubt that an invasion across the English Channel was coming soon; the thing the Germans didn't know was where, and exactly when. Hitler remained convinced that the Allies would try and land in the Pas-de-Calais, the closest point between France and England; it was a reasonable assumption and one that the Allies did their best to confirm. The

Americans fabricated the illusionary First Army Group in south-east England, along with dummy troop camps and phoney dumps. The phantom force even had a real commander, none other than General George S. Patton: meanwhile, the British had also established a fictitious Fourth Army in Scotland, a force poised to fool the Germans into thinking there would be a planned invasion of Norway.

Diversionary attacks in the Pas-de-Calais area were carried out aplenty during the months preceding D-Day,

as were the primary targets to the west. Bridges, roads, railways and fortifications were hit with increasing intensity as were the enemy's airfields. It was still imperative to destroy as much of the Luftwaffe as possible before any cross-Channel invasion and whilst the Eighth continued with its task of daylight raids on strategic targets in Germany, many units now worked alongside the Ninth Air Force, concentrating their efforts on softening up the enemy's ability to resist the forthcoming landings.

WHERE THE EAGLES GATHERED | Robert Taylor

Steve Pisanos, one of the Fourth Fighter Group's most deadly Aces, and fellow P-51B escort pilots quickly break up an attack by Fw190s of JG2 on a B-24 from the 448th Bomb Group.

On Sunday 5 March 1944, a large force of B-24 Liberators set out on one such mission. They included B-24s from the 448th Bomb Group from Seething, whose cover was provided by the one of the finest fighter groups in the Eighth Fighter Command, Colonel Don Blakeslee's famous 'Eagles' – the Fourth Fighter Group based at Debden. The Liberator crews couldn't have asked for better protection, especially as the 'Eagles' had finally transitioned from their heavy and range-restricted P-47s to sleek new long-range P-51 Mustangs.

Typically, however, bad weather hampered the mission.

As often happened over northern France, banks of thick, heavy cloud were rolling in from the Atlantic, obscuring the primary targets. Some revised ones were quickly reassigned whilst the bombers were en-route or, in some cases, simply abandoned. Barely a quarter of the force that set out from England hit enemy airfields, and the Luftwaffe, far from being grounded by the weather, managed to get airborne and into action.

Both sides suffered losses but one was not from enemy action. One of the 'Eagles' up that day was top Fourth Fighter Group Ace, Colonel Steve Pisanos. Flying with the 334th Fighter Squadron he'd had a successful

day tangling with a group of Messerschmitt Bf109 fighters from Jadgeschwader JG2 *Richthofen* as the crack German pilots tried their best to attack the formation of B-24s from the 448th Bomb Group. Pisanos had shot down two of the enemy to bring his tally up to ten aircraft, but they turned out to be his last. On his return flight to England, Pisano's Mustang suffered an engine failure, forcing him to crash-land in northern France where he was picked up by the French Resistance. Instead of being smuggled out of the country to safety, he opted to remain with the Resistance and fought alongside them until he was finally liberated in Paris several months later.

SATURDAY 18 MARCH 44
LAKE CONSTANCE Switzerland
44th Bomb Group

As missions in preparation for D-Day intensified, strategic daylight operations against targets in Germany and Nazi-occupied Europe continued alongside Bomber Command's efforts at night. On Saturday 18 March, whilst Eighth Air Force B-17s pounded aircraft manufacturing and storage facilities elsewhere, more than 200 Second Air Division B-24 Liberators set out on the long ride south to Lake Constance, the boundary between Germany and neutral Switzerland. For the crew of *Sack Artists*, a B-24 from the 506th Bomb Squadron, captained by Bob Cardenas, it was a day they wouldn't forget in a hurry.

Captain Cardenas was Command Pilot for the 44th Bomb Group whose target was an air armaments factory in Friedrichshafen, on the northern shore of the great lake and one known to be heavily defended by flak.

Uncannily the trip south across Germany had been quiet and they'd met little opposition, even though their fighter escort had been delayed. But as they closed on the target they were pounced on from the rear by a large group of enemy fighters. As the formation closed on the target the flak intensified and was worse than expected. A shell tore through *Sack Artist's* starboard wing, ripping it apart and rupturing a fuel line; the fierce explosion

set both right engines on fire. Shards of red-hot, flying shrapnel struck the fuselage wounding several of the crew, including Cardenas who was hit in the head. With his aircraft on fire, the injured Cardenas heaved on the shattered controls – the aircraft somehow responded. The crippled B-24 re-joined the formation to make a second bomb run. *Sack Artists*, however, was in big trouble and rapidly becoming unstable.

With the help of his co-pilot the two men somehow managed to coax the stricken bomber across Lake Constance to neutral Switzerland where Cardenas ordered his crew to bale out. They did so, but for Cardenas the story wasn't over. As he jumped his blossoming parachute was unfortunately caught by a sudden shift of wind and he alone was blown all the way back across the lake to land on its banks – back in Germany. It seemed his luck had finally run out, but the badly wounded Cardenas was having none of it. Determined to avoid capture he plunged into the ice-cold water and swam all the way back to Switzerland where he was interned by the Swiss Air Force.

The story has a happy ending; on 27 September 1944 with the help of Swiss civilians and the French Resistance, Cardenas managed to escape and made it back to England. Returning to the United States he became an instructor and after the war enjoyed a successful career as a highly respected Air Force test pilot.

B-24 SACK ARTISTS | Richard Taylor

LAST MAN OUT | Richard Taylor

Richard Taylor

6 JUNE 1944
D-DAY AND THE EIGHTH

THE FIGHTERS

MONDAY 05 JUNE 44
KINGS CLIFFE Northamptonshire
20th Fighter Group

Two nights had passed since the strange order had been received: ground crews at Kings Cliffe were issued with tins of appropriate paint and instructed to paint black and white stripes around the wings and fuselage booms of the 20th Fighter Group's P-38 Lightnings. The same had happened at the three other Eighth Air Force P-38 stations: the 364th Fighter Group at Honington, the 479th Fighter Group at Wattisham and the 55th Fighter Group at Wormingfold. No explanation had been given, but none was needed, for it soon became apparent that these were the soon-to-be famous 'invasion stripes' allowing friendly aircraft to be easily identified by Allied gunners on the ground and in the air. Within 24 hours all Allied aircraft throughout England involved in

the Normandy Invasion would be similarly adorned.

Alongside their normal escort duties, on D-Day the Eighth's fighters would be dispatched to strafe, harry and dive-bomb any enemy armour or reinforcements seen heading towards the invasion area.

They were also to provide air cover to the invasion fleet. The Eighth's P-38s, along with those from the Ninth, were going to be the first into action because their twin-boom and twin engine silhouette was easily recognisable from the ground by Allied gunners of the

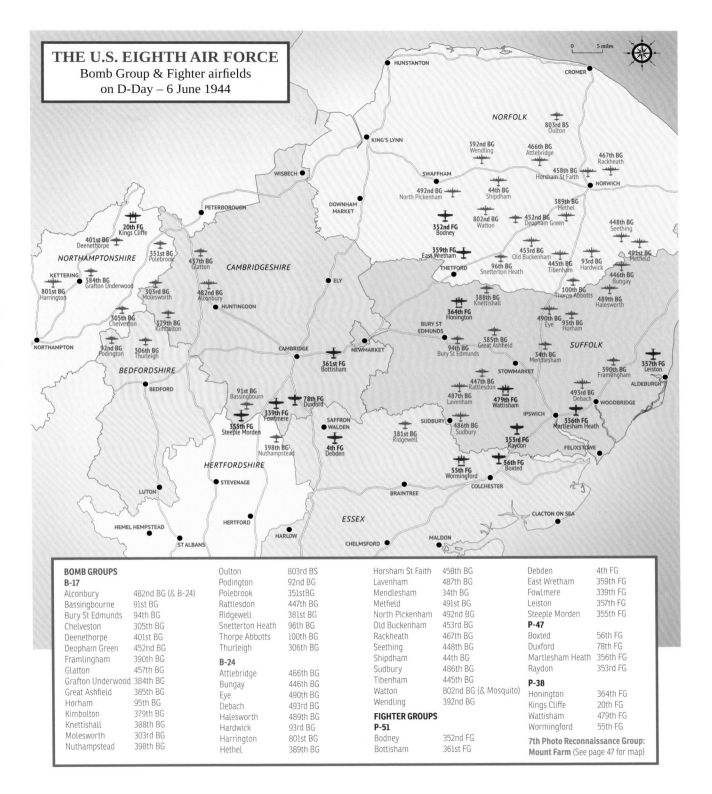

invasion armada. The fleet was vast; nearly 4,500 Allied ships of every conceivable shape and size now stood poised to embark on the greatest amphibious landing the world had ever seen but, for the moment, the weather once again intervened.

A strong storm was blowing up the Channel bringing with it rough seas, high winds and torrential rain. There was no way that landing craft, whose decks were already crammed with sea-sick troops in their sheltered moorings, could attempt a Channel crossing in these conditions. D-Day was postponed for 24 hours.

Early in the morning of 5 June the Supreme Allied Commander, General Eisenhower, faced the most important decision of his life. The weather forecasters were promising him a short lull in the storm – was it long enough to get the fleet across and, more importantly, established? The Germans thought not and thinking an invasion so unlikely, Feldmarshall Erwin Rommel, the famed commander of all German land forces in northern France, took the opportunity to visit his family and celebrate his wife's birthday.

The Germans, however, hadn't reckoned on the accuracy of Eisenhower's resources – or his resolve.

As rain trickled down the windows of his advance headquarters outside Portsmouth, Eisenhower took a deep breath: 'OK' he quietly announced to the officers assembled around him, 'let's go'. The invasion was on.

At 16.51 hours that afternoon, two of the 20th Fighter Group's three squadrons, the 77th and 79th, took off from Kings Cliffe and headed south towards the Solent. The invasion's first patrol was about to begin.

THE FIRST AND THE LAST | Richard Taylor

*Late in the afternoon of D-Day the Eighth flew their fourth
and final mission of the day, targeting German transport
hubs in Normandy. Amongst the bombers dispatched, and
undertaking their first-ever combat mission, were the B-24s
of the 493rd Bomb Group, the last Bomb Group to become
operational with the Eighth.*

THE BOMBERS

TUESDAY 06 JUNE 44
DEBACH Suffolk
493rd Bomb Group

As used as they were to the rumble of heavy aero engines, the night of 5 / 6 June 1944 was something different. In the south and south-west of England, from the late hours onwards, people listened in awe and gazed upwards to witness hundreds upon hundreds of transports towing nearly 1,000 gliders passing overhead. It didn't take much imagination to realise that the big day had finally arrived. The long-expected invasion of Europe was finally underway.

For those living close to an Eighth Air Force airfield in East Anglia, rarely were they woken by the sound of warming engines much before daybreak, but today was unusual. Before the gloomy skies lightened just marginally in the east, the first of over a 1,000 American

bombers began running up their engines, a deafening crescendo that would last for hours.

It was also quite a day on which to undertake your first combat mission, but that was the case for the B-24 Liberator crews of newly-arrived 493rd Bomb Group. Based at RAF Debach in Suffolk, the 493rd Bomb Group – 'Helton's Hellcats' – were the last unit assigned to Eighth Air Force Bomber Command, which had now reached 40 fully operational bomb groups. VIII Bomber Command had reached its zenith.

At first light, in heavy cloud, the Eighth Air Force dispatched a force in excess of 1,300 bombers on missions to attack coastal installations along a wide expanse stretching from Le Havre in the east to Cherbourg to the west. Despite the cloud, and the murk left by the receding storm, most, but not all, managed to find their assigned target.

As the morning rolled on and the landings took hold the Eighth shifted their focus immediately inland. Their next targets were strategic installations in and around the

ancient city of Caen, important transport 'chokepoints' and other communication centres as the Germans tried to rally and rush initial reinforcements to the battle zone. This time the increasing heavy cloud and overcast skies gave the Germans a break – with declining visibility the bombers were finding it difficult to identify their targets. But the weather didn't deter the 'new boys' from the 493rd Bomb Group.

With each bomber bearing the Group's 'Square X' in a square on its vertical stabilisers, the 493rd lifted off from Debach as part of the Eighth's fourth and final mission of the day. They assembled in unison and headed south on a six-and-a-half-hour round trip, again targeting transport hubs serving Normandy. The 493rd went to Liseux, a town 30 miles to the east of Caen on the Paris to Cherbourg railway line where the weather had cleared just enough for them to bomb it successfully, without loss. For the men of 'Helton's Hellcats', their first mission was over.

Keith Burns

DOOLITTLE'S D-DAY | Robert Taylor

TUESDAY 06 JUNE 44
NORMANDY BEACH HEAD

Impatient with not being at the heart of the action and keen to see for himself what was happening in Normandy, Lieutenant General Jimmy Doolittle, Commander of the Eighth Air Force, decided to witness the situation first hand, so he took to the skies. Taking his Deputy Commander Major General 'Pat' Partridge with him as wingman, the two Generals climbed through the clouds and headed south to see how the invasion was progressing – and hoping that the invasion stripes hastily applied to their P-38s would deter the naval gunners! The cloud was thickening but, as they turned for home, inquisitiveness got the better of Doolittle – spotting a break in the overcast he flick-rolled down through it. When 'Pat' Partridge turned his head, having just looked down to change his fuel tanks, Doolittle was nowhere to be seen.

Breaking through the clouds, however, Doolittle now had a grandstand view as one of history's greatest military operations opened up before his eyes. As he flew up and down the battlefront assessing the unfolding events, he witnessed the thousands of ships of all shapes and sizes now well into the process of landing 176,000 troops on the enemy-held beaches. 'It was', he wrote, 'the most impressive and unforgettable sight I could have possibly imagined'.

After a two-and-a-half-hour sortie Doolittle had seen enough and headed back to England. Upon landing he quickly rushed to General Eisenhower's headquarters to provide the Supreme Commander with the first eyewitness report of the day – and in doing so beat the 'official' intelligence by several hours.

D-DAY THE AIRBORNE ASSAULT | Robert Taylor

Closely escorted by P-51s from the 354th Fighter Group, C-47s from the 438th Troop Carrier Wing tow Waco gliders towards the drop zone on the evening of 6 June 1944.

Doolittle could be very proud of his men; between dawn and dusk his heavy bombers had flown well over 2,000 sorties, dropping close to 3,600 tons of bombs. His fighters had performed heroically as well. Flying 1,880 sorties with little sight of enemy fighters, their ground attacks had destroyed huge numbers of targets that included more than 20 locomotives, 85 trains, ammunition wagons, railway sidings, tanks, armoured vehicles and columns of trucks.

BRIDGE BUSTERS | Anthony Saunders

P-47 Thunderbolts from the 78th Fighter Group launch a blistering high-speed, low-level attack, on a German freight train in occupied northern France shortly after D-Day.

TACTICAL SUPPORT

BOSHAM Sussex
364th Fighter Group

Bosham, a dozen or so miles to the west of the great naval base at Portsmouth, is one of the prettiest villages in Sussex. It stands on the tidal, muddy shores of Chichester harbour whose mud flats and intricate little creeks have been home to migrating flocks of wildfowl for centuries. It was here that Canute ordered the waves to retreat, and from the quay close to its ancient Saxon church, Harold had sailed to Normandy in 1064. In June 1944 others from a more modern army sailed from these same shores in a flotilla of landing craft to Gold Beach in Normandy.

The place, quiet as it seemed, was no stranger to the noise of war, especially in the days following D-Day when, amongst many others, the 364th Fighter Group were overhead spectators to these constantly shifting shores and meandering tides. Based at Honington in Suffolk and equipped with Lockheed P-38 Lightnings they'd flown their first combat mission just a mere three months beforehand, escorting the heavies. In the weeks immediately after D-Day they were often seen heading out over the south coast to conduct multiple strafing and ground-attack missions in support of the ground forces

in Normandy. Before long they, like almost every other Eighth Air Force fighter unit, would transition over to long-range North American P-51 Mustangs. The 364th FG would continue to escort the bombers, earning a Distinguished Unit Citation on 27 December 1944 for their role in defending the bombers on a mission to Frankfurt.

SHEPHERD OF THE SEAS

Richard Taylor

DETACHMENT B
65th Fighter Wing (Air-sea Rescue Squadron)

From their first day of operations from England, the Eighth Air Force had relied on the British Royal Navy to help rescue airmen forced to ditch in the Channel or North Sea. That is, if they were fortunate that someone might have picked up their distress call, or they'd been lucky enough to have been spotted in the water.

With more than two years' first-hand experience, particularly during the Battle of Britain, the Royal Air Force had developed sophisticated procedures for air-sea rescues. These involved, amongst other things, specially trained operators to co-ordinate spotter planes, fast motor launches or amphibians that were used in rescue operations, or, failing that, to direct any naval vessels in the vicinity of the unfortunate victim.

But even though cooperation with the RAF was extremely close, in the early days the likelihood of an American airman being safely rescued and returned to dry land was slim – in the first months of 1943 his chances stood at a measly six per cent. As the Eighth Air Force increased in strength and numbers, so too did the number of crews being lost at sea. Increased training in ditching procedures, once again with the help of equipment from the RAF, slowly improved the statistics so that, by the end of the year, nearly 40 per cent of ditched crews now survived.

But in early 1944 the Eighth Air Force High Command concluded it was time to improve that figure

even more by forming an air-sea rescue service of their own. At a meeting between the Eighth Air Force and the RAF it was decided that the 65th Fighter Wing would oversee the establishment of the Eighth's first, and ultimately only, air-sea rescue squadron. The new unit would be commanded by Captain Robert 'Bob' Gerhart from the 56th Fighter Group, and they would be based alongside the 56th FG at Boxted. Eighth Air Force controllers would work alongside their RAF colleagues at Saffron Walden in Essex.

Within a matter of days the resourceful Gerhart had scrounged enough 'war weary' P-47 Thunderbolts from his former Commanding Officer, Colonel 'Hub' Zemke, to equip his new squadron – now officially to be known as 'Detachment B'. The fighters were quickly modified to carry inflatable dinghies under their wings, along with marker buoys and flares.

Obtaining pilots, ground crews and all the other equipment that was needed was another question, but the new commander, with help from Zemke and his staff, attacked the problem with relish. Within a week more than 20 pilots and non-flying officers had been 'loaned' out by other units, along with some 90 supporting ground crew. A new pre-fabricated blister hangar was speedily constructed, and enough equipment begged or borrowed so that, on 10 May, 'Detachment B' flew its first operation. It had been a formidable achievement in so short a period of time, and results were swifter than expected.

On their first day the Eighth's American controllers at Saffron Walden oversaw the successful recovery of a downed fighter pilot from the Fourth Fighter Group rescued by an RAF Walrus amphibian. From now on, whenever a bomber mission departed or, more importantly, returned, a pair of P-47 Thunderbolts from

'Detachment B' would be out on patrol scouting the seas for any ditched crew in need of assistance.

In January 1945, 'Detachment B' moved away from Boxted to new quarters at Halesworth in Suffolk. With the move came a re-designation: they were now to be known as the 5th Emergency Rescue Squadron and, along with their existing P-47s came the arrival of two important new types, Catalina OA-10 amphibians – the Army Air Corps' version of the Navy's PBY Catalina – and B-17 Flying Fortresses carrying airborne lifeboats. Both were pressed into immediate use.

If evidence were ever needed of its usefulness the statistics speak for themselves; by the end of the war 'Detachment B' and the 5th ERS had flown over 3,600 sorties and a total of 938 men had been rescued by their efforts.

SWEET AND LOVELY | Richard Taylor

'Sweet and Lovely', a B-17F serving with the 533rd Bomb Squadron, 381st Bomb Group at Ridgewell. After completing 27 combat missions, 'Sweet and Lovely' was transferred to the 65th Fighter Wing to carry out radio-relay operations over the English Channel.

OUT OF FUEL AND SAFELY HOME | Robert Taylor

TWISTS OF FATE

TUESDAY 11 JULY 44
MUNICH Germany

Munich – the capital of Bavaria and one-time headquarters of Adolf Hitler's Nazi party – had given its name to the infamous treaty in 1938 that ceded Czechoslovakia's Sudetenland to Germany. It was from here that Neville Chamberlain, Britain's Prime Minister, had returned waving the 'piece of paper' that was supposed to bring peace to Europe. It turned out to be an act of appeasement.

Munich was a long way from England but, as the war progressed, the presence of long-range fighter escorts brought it within striking distance of the Eighth's heavy bombers. As the third largest city in Germany it was easy to spot from the air by day and soon became a much-visited and familiar target for the American crews.

The 11 July 1944 mission on targets in and around the Munich area called for maximum effort. All three Eighth Air Force Air Divisions participated in the raid which totalled over 1,200 bombers with nearly 700 escort fighters. For the crew of *Silver Meteor*, a B-17G from the

596th Bomb Squadron, 390th Bomb Group, it began as a routine operation.

First Lieutenant Harry Seip and his crew had flown their first mission at the end of April and were well used to catching sight of distant Framlingham Castle as they departed from their base in the heart of peaceful Suffolk. On that morning everything went smoothly; they'd climbed, assembled, and set their headings south-east for Munich. And much of the trip had been uneventful; the run-in to the target went according to schedule, although the flak and enemy fighters were heavier than anything they'd previously experienced. After releasing their bombs, pilot Harry Seip heaved *Silver Meteor* in an echelon turn along with the rest of the formation and set a course back towards their base in England. Somewhere in the back of his mind were hopes that the second half of the journey would be as quiet as the first – but that was not to be.

Almost immediately after their turn *Silver Meteor* was hit by concentrated and murderous flak bursts. The Fortress began to shake violently as the inner port

WOUNDED WARRIOR | Richard Taylor

THE EAGLES RETURN | Richard Taylor

Ace pilot 'Bud' Anderson in his P-51D 'Old Crow', along with colleagues from the 363rd FS, 357th FG, head back to Leiston after another gruelling escort mission.

engine ground to a standstill and ominously began to smoke. First Lieutenant Seip had no choice but to cut the fuel supply and feather the smoking engine. As their compatriots closed formation, the struggling *Silver Meteor* slipped slowly behind, unable to keep up with the rest of the Group.

The Seip crew now found themselves alone over enemy territory with hundreds of miles to go before they reached the English coastline and, ominously, like sharks scenting blood, enemy fighters had spotted the ailing bomber and began circling, ready to pounce for a quick and easy kill.

But the enemy fighters weren't the only ones who'd spotted the wounded and smoking bomber. Two P-51 Mustangs from the 357th Fighter Group had also seen the prowling German fighters and, with Merlin engines screaming at full throttle, the two P-51 pilots raced to

the scene. The stunned Luftwaffe pilots were quick to sense that both American pilots not only seemed battle-hardened but were experts at their game. The enemy fighters quickly fled.

For Harry Seip and the crew of *Silver Meteor* it was an unbelievably lucky escape but little did they know that the Mustang pilots who'd appeared so miraculously to save their lives were two of the highest-scoring pilots in the Eighth Air Force – Captain C. E. 'Bud' Anderson and Captain Leonard 'Kit' Carson of the 357th Fighter Group – the 'Yoxford Boys'. Thanks to Anderson and Carson's timely intervention, the Seip crew would go on to successfully complete a full combat tour and return to the United States.

THURSDAY 20 JULY 44
Approaching LEIPZIG Saxony

With much of the Luftwaffe's strength in the west now being directed to support German ground forces battling to repel the Allied landings in Normandy, the skies over Germany were left in the hands of a much reduced, yet battle-hardened number of Luftwaffe Day Fighter units. Although lacking overall numbers, it did not halt the ferocity of their 'hit-and-run' assaults on the Eighth's bombers – despite the benefit of the latter's long-range fighter escort.

The Luftwaffe fighter pilots had learnt many lessons over the past year on tactics, attack methods and the vulnerabilities of their American foes. Head-on attacks in massed formations and 'hit-and-run' strikes, although more dangerous, were now common practice for the German fighter pilots.

As part of their 'hit-and-run' tactic the Luftwaffe would assemble as many fighters in one place as they could, then pounce hard and fast from the rear, picking off whatever bombers were in the most vulnerable position. A month before, on 29 June, 37 bombers failed to return from raids targeting synthetic oil plants and aircraft factories at Leipzig, in the eastern state of Saxony.

On 20 July 1944, a day when over 1,000 Eighth Air Force bombers were dispatched to Germany, it was the turn of the 91st Bomb Group and the First Air Division to visit Leipzig once again; their target this time was the airfield at Leipzig-Mockau, one of three sites manufacturing Messerschmitt Bf 109 fighters and the Luftwaffe's revolutionary new Me 262 jet interceptor.

As the formations began to spread out for the bomb run, the 401st Bomb Squadron took the low position – the one most vulnerable to attack. They included *The Peacemaker*, whose bombardier was just checking the bombsight when all hell broke loose – they'd been pounced by Luftwaffe Focke-Wulf Fw 190s. As the enemy fighters ripped into the 91st Bomb Group bombers, *The Peacemaker* was badly hit in the wing and tail by the determined attack, causing the damaged Fortress to stagger and slip behind the rest of the formation. The wounded bomber was still flying, however, unlike their formation leader whose blazing aircraft spun violently down into the void below.

Making the ship as light as possible to keep her in the air, *The Peacemaker's* crew ditched everything that could be jettisoned out of the struggling bomber – including the bombardier's valuable 20lb Norden bombsight – for him the worst moment of the mission. *The Peacemaker* made it safely back to Bassingbourn that day; however, eight Fortresses and their ten-man crews did not.

WELCOME SIGHT | Robert Taylor

"...I suddenly noticed a line of small white puffs ahead of us. At the same moment as my mind registered 'self-destroying cannon shells', one of the crew yelled 'fighters!'. Almost immediately I caught sight of the grey shapes of Focke-Wulfs flashing past and S-ing away down. The next moment our formation leader, afire from one wing tip to the other, slid across our nose. An Fw 190 appeared not more than 200 feet from the left of my window, firing at the bomber ahead. By this time I had reached the nose guns and swung them after him as he dived away. In the turmoil there was no chance to see whether my fire claimed him."

Lt. Marion Havelaar, Bombardier on *The Peacemaker*

BRINGING THE PEACEMAKER HOME | Robert Taylor

— 27 —

Robert Taylor

THE JET THREAT

FRIDAY 28 JULY 44
Departing MERSEBURG Saxony

Allied planners suspected that Leipzig-Mockau airfield, the target visited by the 91st Bomb Group a few days earlier, was harbouring Messerschmitt's new Me 262, the jet interceptor they feared would soon strike the Allied bomber formations. But the new 'fighter' that the bomber crews briefly caught sight of was altogether something else. The stunned airmen could scarcely register the fact that diving through their midst, at speeds hitherto unimaginable for any aircraft, was a small

formation of short, stubby, tail-less bee-like machines with swept wings. The black crosses on the wings and swastika on the tail, however, were very familiar!

With a limited flight time of only seven or eight minutes the encounter was over within seconds and no damage was done, but the Eighth Air Force had had its first glimpse of the Nazi's new 'rocket' plane – the Messerschmitt Me 163 *Komet*.

The Me 163s belonged to *Erprobungskommando 16*, a testing unit commanded by top Luftwaffe Ace Major Wolfgang Späte. His unit of Me 163 *Komets* would shortly become Jagdgeschwader JG400. Coming as it did just a few days after their first sighting of a Me 262 jet fighter, the American bomber crews had yet another new threat to deal with and, in the months ahead, the level of that threat would become substantial.

BRIEF ENCOUNTER | Richard Taylor ▶

Despite speeds far in excess of any Allied fighter, the Luftwaffe's revolutionary rocket-powered Me 163 Komet was hindered by lack of range and a measly flight time restricted to a few brief minutes. Though outrageously fast, the Me 163 proved ineffective in action and is thought to have destroyed only a dozen or so Allied aircraft.

MONDAY 28 AUGUST 44
19.15 hrs BELGIUM
78th Fighter Group

The new Me 262 jet had grabbed the attention of Eighth Air Force Command but few had either seen or encountered it in combat. So when Major Joseph Myers and his compatriots in the 78th Fighter Group's 82nd Fighter Squadron first spotted the twin-engine aircraft flying beneath them over the Belgian countryside, at first they assumed it was an American B-26 Marauder – except this particular aircraft was flying far too fast.

Diving to investigate, Myers quickly realised that the mystery aircraft was none other the Luftwaffe's new jet. Myers was in luck because unknown to him, the jet was unarmed and preparing to land. It was being moved on a short-hop 200 km ferry flight from Juvincourt near Rheims in France to Chièvres, and the pilot was Oberfeldwebel 'Ronnie' Lauer.

Lauer was no inexperienced rookie. He'd quickly spotted the 78th Fighter Group Thunderbolts diving behind him at high speed but Lauer was in a vulnerable position; he was far too low to make any evasive manoeuvre to escape. He did what he could to flee the pursuing Thunderbolts but his wing-tip struck the ground and he crash-landed his jet near the airfield. Major Myers, along with his wingman, Lieutenant Manford Croy, circled around and strafed the burning jet, totally destroying it in a ball of fire. Lauer escaped the crash and lived to fight another day – he later took part in the famous jet attacks on the bridge at Remagen. Major Myers and Lieutenant Croy claimed the victory nonetheless. It was the Eighth's first victory over the German Me 262.

THE MIGHTY EIGHTH – OUTWARD BOUND | Robert Taylor

The old and battle-weary B-24D 'The Little Gramper' acted as the assembly ship for the 491st Bomb Group at North Pickenham.

AUGUST 44
486th / 487th Bomb Groups

The Eighth Air Force has, in popular mythology, been closely associated with the magnificent B-17 Flying Fortress but ever since the end of 1943 there had been a steady increase in the number of Eighth Air Force Bomb Groups equipped with B-24s. Ten such units had become operational since the beginning of the year.

But there were problems, not in the capabilities of either aircraft because each had loyal and dogged admirers, but because the two types could never work effectively alongside each other. The two types not only had different cruising speeds, but operated better at differing altitudes.

Of the Eighth's three Air Divisions, the First Air Division solely operated B-17s and the Second Air Division was equipped with B-24s. The Third Air Division, however, flew both types. It was therefore decided to convert all of the Third's five B-24 groups over to the B-17.

By the beginning of August both the 486th and 487th Bomb Groups had made the transition over to Fortresses and flown their first missions with them. The three remaining Third Air Division B-24 groups, the 34th BG, 490th BG and 493rd BG, would complete their own transitions within a matter of weeks. Nevertheless, with the Second Air Division remaining an all-Liberator unit, B-24s continued to equip roughly a third of the Eighth's heavy bomber strength.

BRIGHT, GAUDY AND UNMISSABLE

The Assembly Ships

The doctrine of precision daylight bombing hinged on precision flying, and no one was better at keeping formation than the B-17 and B-24 pilots of the Eighth Air Force. They needed to be the best because their lives, and those of their crews, depended on it.

Flying a bomber in daylight over enemy skies was asking for trouble and many of the tactics designed to offset some of the danger had been pioneered by Curtis LeMay, then a Colonel and the original Commander of the 305th Bomb Group based at Chelveston. The most important by far was the 'combat box' – a tightly organised, yet complex staggered formation of bombers that provided two things: defensively it maximised the amount of firepower that could be brought to bear at any one time against an attacker and, offensively, provided everyone held their course and only released their bombs when instructed to do so by the master bombardier in the lead aircraft, bombs were concentrated more accurately on target. These 'combat boxes' proved successful in the early days and would be later refined as the war progressed.

Getting into the correct position in the first place, however, was a task in itself. The procedure required the help of 'Judas Goats', war-weary bombers equipped with signal lamps and brightly coloured flares, and painted in outlandish, yet unmissable, colour schemes upon which the various squadrons and groups could establish their correct formations.

With black humour the airmen called these psychedelic creations 'Judas Goats', goats trained by shepherds to befriend sheep before leading them off – usually to slaughter.

THUNDERHEADS OVER RIDGEWELL | Robert Taylor

Anthony Saunders

SATURATED BY FLAK

MONDAY 11 SEPTEMBER 44

MERSEBURG Saxony

Whilst the names of Schweinfurt, Regensburg and Berlin had come to be feared as heavily defended targets, and dreaded by the Eighth's heavy bomber crews, by the autumn of 1944 the name most never wanted to hear was Merseburg. Whenever the name was mentioned as the target of the day an audible, collective sigh of dismay was sent through many a briefing room.

Situated close to Leipzig in the far east of Germany, about a hundred miles south-east of Berlin, Merseburg was home to some of the Third Reich's leading manufacturers of chemicals, whilst a few miles away in the southern suburbs lay the synthetic oil plant of Leuna. This sprawling complex, one of the largest of its kind in the world, processed abundant supplies of locally mined lignite into synthetic oil, the essential ingredient that was needed to power the machinery of the German armed forces. The fuel manufactured at Leuna accounted for about 10% of the Reich's output, but that wasn't all it produced; the site also manufactured a large quantity of chemicals, including half of the ammonium nitrate used in German explosives and deuterium oxide, the 'heavy water' essential for Hitler's secret plans to develop an atomic bomb.

Having scant reliable access to natural oil, German scientists had been, and still were, world leaders at converting its abundant seams of black coal and lignite into oil and Hitler's pre-war Nazi government was instrumental in developing increased production, with generous financial help from the state. The party was already planning for war; by the outbreak of hostilities synthetic oil plants had been constructed right across the country, but the most important was at Leuna.

By the summer of 1944, Germany's need for gasoline and the high quality aviation fuel in which it specialised, including that used in their new jet engines, had become critical. Merseburg, and the surrounding plants in the region, had made it to the top of the list of 'priority targets' for Eighth Air Force Bomber Command.

Despite the constant bombing of factories involved with fighter production and the fact that in the air the Eighth Air Force were winning the war for air supremacy, the Luftwaffe remained deadly opponents and could still field hundreds of fighters in defence of their oil facilities. Their revolutionary Me 262 jets and Me 163 rocket fighters had already been encountered in the Leipzig / Merseberg area. But it wasn't the fighters the

Ol' GAPPY - RIDING THE FLAK | Richard Taylor

The air is alive with deadly explosions as 'Ol Gappy' and the B-17s of the 524th Bomb Squadron, 379th Bomb Group run into the intense flak over Merseburg, 11 September 1944.

bomber crews feared the most – their fighter escorts helped with that threat; it was the daunting German anti-aircraft defences. And, given its importance, the region had become the most heavily-defended location in what remained of Hitler's teetering Reich. Amongst Eighth Air Force bomber crews Merseberg was simply known as 'flak city'.

By the second half of 1944 over a thousand flak guns, many of them radar-controlled, had been grouped into a series of powerful batteries positioned around Leipzig, double the number of those protecting the capital, Berlin. More than half of this firepower defended Merseburg / Leuna, including huge 125mm anti-aircraft guns that delivered shells with such explosive power that they could bring down an aircraft from a hundred yards without hitting it. The sky, according to the crews that flew through it, was literally 'saturated' by German flak.

The Eighth flew a score of missions to Merseburg, including one on 11 September when it dispatched over 1,100 heavy bombers, with a large long-range fighter escort, to attack as many oil plants across Germany as it could, along with other targets.

Merseburg was scheduled to receive a visit from a large part of that force.

Ol Gappy, a B-17G Flying Fortress from the 524th Bomb Squadron, 379th Bomb Group was a 'lucky' Fortress, one that survived until the end of the war and completed 157 combat operations, believed to be more than any other bomber in the Eighth. Today *Ol Gappy* and the rest of the 379th were going to Meresburg.

Briefing at Kimbolton had been a tense affair. In spite of the nervous laughter and black humour every crew in the room was aware that today's mission was going to be a tough one. Some of the familiar faces around them might not be coming home.

And so it proved. During the day 40 bombers and 17 of their escort fighters would be lost.

By the end of hostilities the 379th Bomb Group had flown more sorties and dropped a greater tonnage of bombs than any other group in the Eighth Air Force. If only *Ol Gappy's* last days had had the ending worthy of her service. In all her record-breaking missions she'd only had to turn back once but, within months of the war's end she was sent back to America, where she would be sold off for scrap.

"An overall shortage of aviation gasoline," reported the United States Strategic Bombing Survey, *"resulted in the curtailment of flying training as early as 1942 and this decision was reflected in a deterioration of quality of personnel, which was the principal cause of the defeat of the German Air Force."*
Dr Kenneth Werrell, Air University Review

CO-OPERATION | Keith Burns

A WELCOME RETURN | Anthony Saunders

TUESDAY 21 NOVEMBER
MERSEBURG Saxony
352nd Fighter Group

Once again the Eighth's bombers were heading to Germany and a large part of that force was aiming for targets in and around the Merseburg / Leuna area. For the bomber crews, they knew it would prove to be a hell of a day battling the heavy flak around the oil plants they intended to hit. There was little doubt they would also encounter enemy fighters along the route. German fighter attacks had been increasing in intensity but, hopefully, the large number of P-51 Mustangs escorting them could deal with at least some of opposition. What no-one expected,

however, was the scale of the day's Luftwaffe presence. It was huge.

Luftwaffe losses over Meresburg in the weeks beforehand had been significant but the Germans weren't ready to throw in the towel – at least not yet. On 21 November the Luftwaffe had gathered enough units together to launch the first of three major operations, a last, ultimately vain attempt to halt what was developing into a one-sided losing battle. From the outset the day didn't go well for them.

Some Focke-Wulf Fw 190 units were late on the scene when the P-51s Mustangs caught them off-guard, some still assembling in cloud banks to the west of the target area. Prominent alongside the 'green-nosed' Mustangs of the 359th Fighter Group were the distinctive 'blue noses' of the 352nd Fighter Group, the famous 'Blue-Nosed Bastards of Bodney', whose numbers today included the Eighth's top-scoring P-51 Ace, Major George E. Preddy.

Preddy and the other pilots of the 352nd FG were initially surprised by the lack of experience shown by some of the Luftwaffe pilots. Not that it mattered because the Mustang pilots were about to embark on a field day. In an almost one-sided engagement, which quickly developed into a dramatic chase across the cold winter skies, no less than 73 enemy fighters were shot down, for the loss of just two P-51s. For the Luftwaffe the battle had been nothing short of a rout and over the next few days, as their losses mounted, any hopes that their fighters could stage some kind of miraculous comeback were dashed.

Led by their Commanding Officer Major George Preddy, P-51 pilots of the 328th FS, 352nd Fighter Group engage in a bitter struggle with Fw 190s high over Merseburg, eastern Germany, November 1944.

The 'Blue-Nosed Bastards of Bodney'
352nd Fighter Group

An outstanding collection of talented pilots served in the three squadrons that comprised the 352nd Fighter Group – the 328th, 486th and 487th Fighter Squadrons. By the end of the war their numbers included 29 of the USAAF's top air Aces in Europe, five of whom, including Major George E. Preddy, had achieved the status of becoming an 'Ace in a Day' – the near-miraculous feat of shooting down five or more enemy aircraft in a single day was truly remarkable – and the 352nd Fighter Group had more 'Aces in a Day' than any other Eighth Air Force Group. And it wasn't just against piston-engine fighters that the Group had success: twelve 352nd FG pilots scored aerial victories over the fast and revolutionary German jets.

Major 'Bill' Whisner, who'd once served as Preddy's wingman, was one of the few fighter pilots to become an Ace in both WWII and in Korea whilst another 352nd Ace – Lt. Col John C. Meyer, a one-time commander of the 487th Fighter Squadron – achieved 24 victories in air combat. It made him the seventh highest Allied Ace of the war. The 487th Fighter Squadron also happened to be the only individual fighter squadron in the Eighth Air Force to be awarded a Distinguished Unit Citation – for actions on 1 January 1945 when they destroyed 23 enemy aircraft during the German air offensive *Operation Bodenplatte*.

Major George E. Preddy 352nd Fighter Group
Highest scoring Mustang Ace in the Eighth

Richard Taylor

Highly decorated and the top-scoring Mustang Ace in the Eighth Air Force, for George Preddy disaster struck on Christmas Day 1944 when he was tragically killed in action. Ironically his P-51 was hit by friendly fire from U.S. anti-aircraft guns close to the frontline in Belgium.

After seeing service in the Pacific flying P-40s with the 49th Fighter Group in defence of northern Australia, he was assigned to the 352nd Fighter Group and arrived in England during the summer of 1943. Based at Bodney airfield in Norfolk he flew a tour with the 487th Fighter Squadron during which time, on 6 August 1944, he downed no less than six Luftwaffe Messerschmitt Bf109s in a day. After a brief spell away from combat in the United States, he returned for a second tour with the 352nd in October 1944. Preddy was promoted to the rank of Major and was given command of the 328th Fighter Squadron.

With his personal aircraft, emblazoned with the nickname 'Cripes A'Mighty', his final mission came on 25 December 1944. It would be Preddy's 143rd mission of the war, during which time he'd achieved his impressive tally of 25 aircraft destroyed plus an additional four shared aerial victories.

HOME RUN | Robert Taylor

'LITTLE FRIENDS'

The heavy bomber losses amassed by the Eighth's long-distance, unescorted daylight missions during the latter half of 1943 hadn't been forgotten, but they had been markedly reduced, thanks partly to improved tactics, better radar and electronic counter-measures and aircraft defensive improvements. But the main reason for a reduction in the scale of losses had been the introduction of long-range fighters equipped with external drop tanks. However, even with the addition of long-range fuel tanks, the Eighth Air Force P-47s and P-38s struggled to make it all the way to the deep penetration targets. It was only when the first North American P-51 Mustangs appeared in the theatre and became operational, was the problem finally resolved. And it didn't take long for the sleek new fighter to turn the tables on the Luftwaffe, establishing itself as probably the best all-round fighter of the war.

Ironically the U.S. Army Air Corps hadn't been impressed with North American's new creation and refused to endorse or pay for its development. It was the Royal Air Force who saved the day for the Mustang and started production, albeit with an underpowered

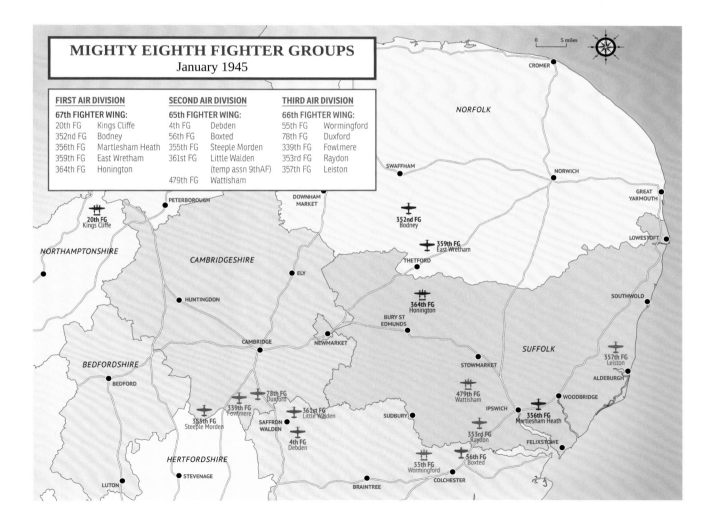

MIGHTY EIGHTH FIGHTER GROUPS
January 1945

FIRST AIR DIVISION	SECOND AIR DIVISION	THIRD AIR DIVISION
67th FIGHTER WING:	**65th FIGHTER WING:**	**66th FIGHTER WING:**
20th FG — Kings Cliffe	4th FG — Debden	55th FG — Wormingford
352nd FG — Bodney	56th FG — Boxted	78th FG — Duxford
356th FG — Martlesham Heath	355th FG — Steeple Morden	339th FG — Fowlmere
359th FG — East Wretham	361st FG — Little Walden	353rd FG — Raydon
364th FG — Honington	(temp assn 9thAF)	357th FG — Leiston
	479th FG — Wattisham	

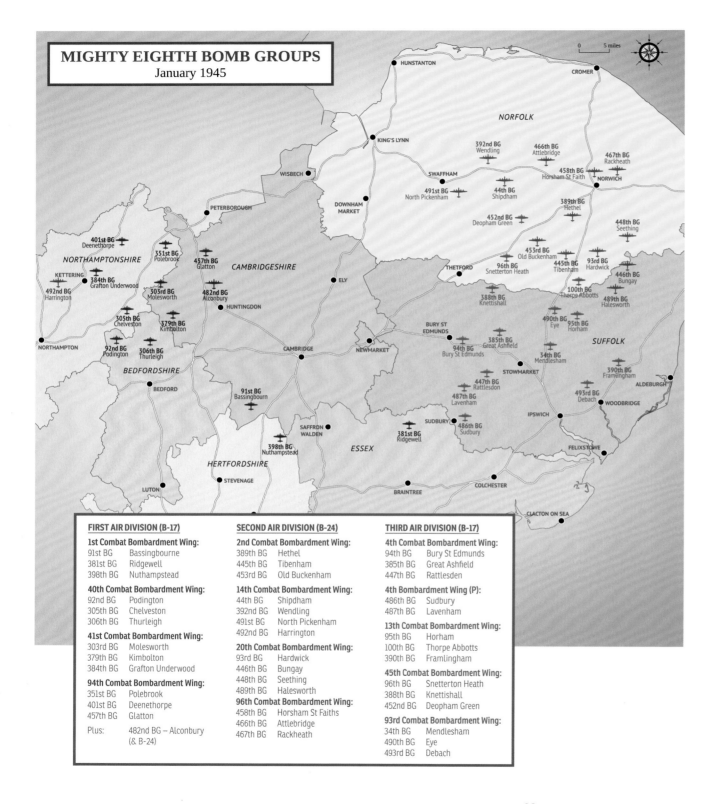

MIGHTY EIGHTH BOMB GROUPS
January 1945

0   5 miles

HUNSTANTON

CROMER

NORFOLK

KING'S LYNN

392nd BG
Wendling

466th BG
Attlebridge

467th BG
Rackheath

WISBECH

SWAFFHAM

458th BG
Horsham St Faith

NORWICH

PETERBOROUGH

DOWNHAM
MARKET

491st BG
North Pickenham

44th BG
Shipdham

389th BG
Hethel

448th BG
Seething

401st BG
Deenethorpe

351st BG
Polebrook

457th BG
Glatton

CAMBRIDGESHIRE

452nd BG
Deopham Green

NORTHAMPTONSHIRE

ELY

453rd BG
Old Buckenham

445th BG
Tibenham

93rd BG
Hardwick

446th BG
Bungay

KETTERING

384th BG
Grafton Underwood

303rd BG
Molesworth

482nd BG
Alconbury

THETFORD

96th BG
Snetterton Heath

100th BG
Thorpe Abbotts

489th BG
Halesworth

492nd BG
Harrington

HUNTINGDON

388th BG
Knettishall

305th BG
Chelveston

379th BG
Kimbolton

490th BG
Eye

95th BG
Horham

NORTHAMPTON

92nd BG
Podington

306th BG
Thurleigh

CAMBRIDGE

NEWMARKET

BURY ST
EDMUNDS

385th BG
Great Ashfield

94th BG
Bury St Edmunds

34th BG
Mendlesham

SUFFOLK

BEDFORDSHIRE

BEDFORD

STOWMARKET

390th BG
Framlingham

ALDEBURGH

91st BG
Bassingbourn

447th BG
Rattlesden

487th BG
Lavenham

493rd BG
Debach

WOODBRIDGE

IPSWICH

SAFFRON
WALDEN

SUDBURY

486th BG
Sudbury

FELIXSTOWE

398th BG
Nuthampstead

ESSEX

381st BG
Ridgewell

HERTFORDSHIRE

LUTON

STEVENAGE

BRAINTREE

COLCHESTER

CLACTON ON SEA

FIRST AIR DIVISION (B-17)		SECOND AIR DIVISION (B-24)		THIRD AIR DIVISION (B-17)	
1st Combat Bombardment Wing:		**2nd Combat Bombardment Wing:**		**4th Combat Bombardment Wing:**	
91st BG	Bassingbourne	389th BG	Hethel	94th BG	Bury St Edmunds
381st BG	Ridgewell	445th BG	Tibenham	385th BG	Great Ashfield
398th BG	Nuthampstead	453rd BG	Old Buckenham	447th BG	Rattlesden
40th Combat Bombardment Wing:		**14th Combat Bombardment Wing:**		**4th Bombardment Wing (P):**	
92nd BG	Podington	44th BG	Shipdham	486th BG	Sudbury
305th BG	Chelveston	392nd BG	Wendling	487th BG	Lavenham
306th BG	Thurleigh	491st BG	North Pickenham	**13th Combat Bombardment Wing:**	
41st Combat Bombardment Wing:		492nd BG	Harrington	95th BG	Horham
303rd BG	Molesworth	**20th Combat Bombardment Wing:**		100th BG	Thorpe Abbotts
379th BG	Kimbolton	93rd BG	Hardwick	390th BG	Framlingham
384th BG	Grafton Underwood	446th BG	Bungay	**45th Combat Bombardment Wing:**	
94th Combat Bombardment Wing:		448th BG	Seething	96th BG	Snetterton Heath
351st BG	Polebrook	489th BG	Halesworth	388th BG	Knettishall
401st BG	Deenethorpe	**96th Combat Bombardment Wing:**		452nd BG	Deopham Green
457th BG	Glatton	458th BG	Horsham St Faiths	**93rd Combat Bombardment Wing:**	
Plus:	482nd BG – Alconbury	466th BG	Attlebridge	34th BG	Mendlesham
	(& B-24)	467th BG	Rackheath	490th BG	Eye
				493rd BG	Debach

Alison engine. But once Rolls-Royce had strapped one of its magical Merlin engines in place, the Mustang was transformed from workhorse into thoroughbred. Eighth Air Force Fighter Command had the answer to its prayers. During the pre-invasion period earlier in the year the Eighth's fighters had already made serious inroads into the Luftwaffe's once-held supremacy of the European skies. The tables had turned by summer and now, as winter crept ever nearer, it was not only air superiority that the Eighth held, but numerical superiority as well. The slick, well-oiled and well-managed production lines that had made America such a formidable industrial power, were now turning out bombers and fighters at an unbeatable rate. Even in peacetime it would have been a challenge for the factories of the Third Reich to compete with such manufacturing prowess. But in war, with its industry throttled and disintegrating under the weight of Allied bombs, it was impossible. All that Germany could hope for was that their remarkable talent for innovation could save the day.

LITTLE FRIENDS | Robert Taylor

*P-51s of the 20th Fighter Group provide close support for 'Bit-O-Lace',
the B-17 having sustained severe flak damage over Kiel, Germany.*

*P-51s of the 78th Fighter Group return to Duxford following an
8 hour escort mission during the cold winter of 1944-45.*

BITTER MID-WINTER

The winter of 1944 / 45 wasn't the coldest ever
recorded in England, but it came close. The weather
was bleak and bitter and, in what would turn out to be the
last Christmas of the war, temperatures plunged across
the country, bringing ice, freezing fog and deep banks of
drifting snow. Familiar carols were once again sung and,
for this Christmas at least, the earth did stand 'hard as
iron, water like a stone'.

But there were few glad tidings, little comfort or
joy, and certainly no peace on earth. Regardless of either
religion or the weather, the war went on regardless. The
end game was approaching, and both sides knew it.

As Christmas approached a score of airfields across
East Anglia stood bleak and frost-bound. The Eighth Air
Force was grounded. Runways kept clear of snow when
conditions allowed, and the bombers remained under
wraps, engines oiled, warmed and ready for any break in
the banks of murky freezing fog that would allow them
to fly. When those breaks in the weather came, the Eighth
Air Force went back into action.

SUNDAY 24 DECEMBER 44
Nr. LUDWIGSLUST Germany

The sunless, dreary skies that had cast their frosty
shadow over much of north-west Europe for days were
beginning to lift. The weather forecasters had predicted
clear skies beginning on 24 December, Christmas Eve.
On that day the Eighth Air Force launched a 'maximum
effort' mission, a force of 2,034 heavy bombers, along
with 853 escorting fighters. It was part of the largest
single operation carried out by the Allied air forces in
World War II.

Almost every bomber capable of flight was pressed
into service – even a few, hastily-re-armed 'Judas Goats'
got in on the action. In support, RAF Bomber Command
and the Ninth Air Force contributed another 500 or so
heavy bombers to the day's missions – to attack airfields,
marshalling yards and other centres of communications
across the breadth of western Germany. The force flew in
support of the Allied ground forces battling to staunch the
Wehrmacht's savage and unexpected thrust through the

Richard Taylor

Ardennes that had begun just over a week before.

It was a successful mission only dampened, once
again, by deteriorating weather. The clear blue, wintry
skies that had enabled the bombers to get airborne in
the morning had conspired to create layers of familiar
haze and fog as they returned to their bases in England,
obscuring some of the more inland airfields. Tired crews,
with their bombers low on fuel, put down at wherever

FORTRESS AT REST | Richard Taylor

*Deep overnight snow at RAF Nuthampstead temporarily
grounds the B-17s of the 398th Bomb Group.*

base they could see and many woke on Christmas Day to
unfamiliar surroundings. Ridgewell, for example, home
to the 381st Bomb Group, had remained clear of fog all
day and was now jam-packed with nearly 80 additional
bombers from other groups.

Although a great success for the Eighth Air Force,
the Christmas Eve mission saw them lose one their
greatest combat commanders – Brigadier General

Frederick Walker Castle. As Commanding Officer,
Castle had turned the 94th Bomb Group into one of the
best groups in the Third Air Division before assuming
command of the Fourth Combat Bomb Wing in April
1944, and was soon promoted to Brigadier General at the
age of 36.

When the orders for the Christmas Eve mission
came through, Castle decided to lead his Bomb Wing.
Flying with the 487th Bomb Group from Lavenham,
he flew as co-pilot and mission commander on the lead
aircraft. The mission fell behind due to the weather and

the 487th BG missed the rendezvous with their P-51
Mustang escort over the Continent. German fighters
soon pounced on the unprotected formation and Castle's
bomber was badly hit in the attack, crippling its ability
to stay with the rest of the formation. The damaged B-17
soon fell behind and was once again struck by enemy
fighters, the attack setting ablaze the bomber's two
starboard engines. Castle ordered the Deputy Commander
to take over the mission lead, and his own crew to bail
out of the burning Fortress.

As the blazing aircraft spun rapidly earthward, seven of the nine crew somehow managed to get out. The pilot was last seen strapping on his parachute whilst Castle remained resolute at the controls trying to steady the ship as much as possible. Suddenly, the fuel tank in the bomber's right wing exploded, sending the aircraft into a violent and terrifying spin before hitting the ground in a wooded area near Hods in Belgium. Both General Castle and the pilot were killed.

For his bravery and undaunted courage that day, Brigadier General Castle was awarded the Medal of Honor.

WINTER'S WELCOME | Robert Taylor

Robert Taylor

SAVAGE SKIES

SUNDAY 31 DECEMBER 44
Nr. KOBLENZ Germany

Weather conditions by New Year's Eve were little better. A series of blizzards swept across the frozen landscape, the biting wind freezing hands and faces and penetrating every crack and crevice in barely warm huts that the airmen called 'home'. Once again the Eighth Air Force was virtually grounded.

Meanwhile, three hundred miles away in the Ardennes Forest, hard-pressed German troops were mounting a stiffer than expected resistance in the closing stages of the 'Battle of the Bulge' – a surprise offensive executed by the Germans two weeks earlier. As the Allied armies tried to recover the momentum they'd lost after

the enemy's unexpected offensive, the air campaign was stalled by the dismal weather conditions.

By this stage of the war the Luftwaffe had, by and large, long since surrendered air superiority but that didn't mean they'd stopped fighting – far from it. As with the German Army's counter-offensive on the ground, the Luftwaffe had their surprise in store as events later in the day would prove.

But with the morning light growing brighter amidst the gloom, the Eighth Air Force continued their missions on 31 December. Over 1,300 bombers, with nearly 800 fighter escorts, once again lumbered off the frozen runways of their English bases to head east to their designated targets. A large force of B-17s headed for various oil refineries and storage facilities in and around

Hamburg, others targeted communication centres and bridges, including the one at Remagen. Similar targets awaited the third group, this time made up of Liberators from the Second Air Division, including those of the 453rd Bomb Group whose four squadrons were based at Old Buckenham in Norfolk.

The 453rd BG had been tasked with destroying the graceful spans of the Güls Railway Bridge over the Moselle, just outside Koblenz. This vital target was a strategic link in a rail line running from Berlin to western Germany. The outbound journey from England had gone reasonably well; the Liberator crews hoped that the bad weather might keep the enemy fighters grounded. As the American formation embarked on their final bomb run, however, the enemy fighters pounced.

German ground radar had detected the force of incoming Liberators in time to get a force of sleek, long-nose Focke-Wulf Fw 190D-9s from III./JG54 airborne to unleash a defensive attack.

Part of the elite 'Green Hearts' Gruppe commanded by top Ace Dieter Hrabak, they were the first group in the Luftwaffe to be equipped with Focke-Wulf's newest, highly potent high-altitude 'long nose' version of its famous Fw 190 fighter. Along with the Me 262 jet, the

Fw 190D-9 'Doras' were one fighter the B-24s didn't want to tangle with. Luckily for the 453rd Bomb Group, their ever-present P-51 escorts were quickly dispatched to the scene to drive the German attackers off. Although several were badly damaged, some beyond repair, the formation of Liberators escaped loss.

It transpired that the Luftwaffe was saving itself for their own big surprise the following day.

SAVAGE SKIES | Robert Taylor

Whilst German troops battle with Allied ground forces advancing through several inches of snow in the Ardennes, a formation of Fw 190D-9 fighters from 12./JG54 attack 453rd Bomb Group B-24s from the 2nd Air Division south of Koblenz, Germany. Some 6,000 feet above, top-cover P-51 Mustangs dive to the Liberators' assistance, 31 December 1944.

THE LEGEND OF Y-29 ASCHE

When Alan Turing and the code-breakers at Bletchley Park finally cracked the German Enigma ciphers in 1941, Allied Intelligence held a priceless advantage for the rest of the war. General Eisenhower later wrote that the intelligence gathered at Bletchley had "saved countless British and American lives and, in no small way, contributed to the speed with which the enemy was routed and eventually forced to surrender".

No one, however, had foreseen or been fore-warned of the German counter-offensive on 16 December 1944 through the Ardennes. Allied intelligence knew something was afoot with the Germans but its imminence was dismissed, After all, how could the enemy gather together three armies, elite SS units, and a quarter of a million men without the Allies knowing? But, behind a veil of total secrecy, that was exactly what the Germans had done; and they'd done it with speed and guile, launching their vicious attack in the one part of the front line that no one thought possible; a quiet backwater, the dense forests of the Ardennes.

The German plan called for a lightning thrust, one that would carry the panzers all the way to Antwerp, thereby splitting the forces of the American, British and Canadian armies in two. Now, in the snow-bound town of Bastogne, U.S. Airborne Divisions were surrounded, fighting for their lives as they attempted to staunch the tide.

The Luftwaffe now sprang their own surprise; drawing on units from the east, they planned a mass assault on the Allies' advance airfields set up in the Low Countries. The build-up also went unnoticed – until at dawn on New Year's Day when the Luftwaffe unleashed 'Operation Bodenplatte'.

The airfield at Asch in Belgium was home to the Ninth Air Force's 366th Fighter Group, equipped with P-47 Thunderbolts. Also on the temporary base were P-51 Mustangs of the Eighth's 352nd Fighter Group, who were operating alongside the Thunderbolts of the Ninth Air Force.

BEYOND THE STORM | Anthony Saunders

Flying his P-51D 'Miss Helen', Captain Ray Littge leads 487th Fighter Squadron, 352nd Fighter Group Mustangs home after a bomber escort mission to Germany.

THE LEGEND OF ASCH | Richard Taylor

Under fire and with his gear still retracting, Lt. Col. John C. Meyer opens fire to score a victory as he takes to the air leading the 487th Fighter Squadron, 352nd Fighter Group into action against the surprise Luftwaffe attack on Y-29 Airfield near Asch, Belgium during 'Operation Bodenplatte'.

A patrol of Thunderbolts from the 390th Fighter Squadron was already in the air when the Luftwaffe struck. In an all-out mass attack, dozens of German fighters screamed over the airfield at low-level, just as a dozen Mustangs from the 487th Fighter Squadron led by Lieutenant Colonel John C. Meyer were preparing to get airborne. Meyer's fighters managed to scramble off the makeshift airfield and so began the 'Legend of Asch' – a 45-minute battle that saw 11 of the 12 Mustang pilots score victories as the enemy lost 28 fighters. The 352nd Fighter Group escaped completely unscathed.

It was a rare moment of success in a day when hundreds of Allied aircraft were destroyed on the ground. For the Luftwaffe, however, the victory was pyrrhic. Only a small number of Allied pilots had been lost; most had been on the ground when the attacks began, and whilst their aircraft could be replaced – they were ready within a week – the Luftwaffe had no such reserves. But, more important than the machines was the number of German pilots who'd been killed, wounded or taken prisoner, because they were irreplaceable.

*Luftwaffe fighters from JG300 and JG301 make a head-on attack through a close
formation of B-17s from the 390th Bomb Group near Ludwigslust on 4 January 1945.
But their ever-vigilant P-51 escorts quickly engage the enemy with devastating results.*

Robert Taylor

HEADLONG INTO THE CLASH

SUNDAY 14 JANUARY 45
Nr. LUDWIGSLUST Germany

Despite the cold and unforgiving weather, the
Eighth Air Force continued to press on with their
'maximum effort' offensive to defeat the Luftwaffe and
conclude hostilities. Christmas had passed but the snow
had not, yet the Eighth Air Force bomber bases in East
Anglia still had to operate; runways had to be cleared
and aircraft maintained and prepared for combat. It was
grim, unpleasant but essential work with no let-up for
the ground crews. However, for Germany the war was
going badly and every day in action would bring the war
closer to an end. The noose around the enemy's neck was
tightening.

On their own bomb-scarred, icy airfields the
remnants of the Luftwaffe prepared for the final

onslaught. They might be battered but they hadn't
stopped fighting, not by a long way. Today was no
exception.

For once the bad weather that had so frustrated the
Eighth was forecast to remain clear over the European
continent. In their first major mission of the year, they
had managed to get well over 600 bombers, and almost as
many fighters, into the air. Once again their targets were
the oil refineries and storage depots located in central
Germany. With clear blue skies forecast, the Luftwaffe
was expected to appear in large numbers and they didn't
disappoint. German ground control radar alerted several
Luftwaffe Jagdgeschwaders of the approaching force
and the fighter units had enough time to assemble several
hundred fighters. However even that number wasn't
enough. Numerically overpowered by the strong force of

escorting American Mustangs, the only Eighth Air Force
Bomb Group to sustain serious losses was the 390th
BG, whose low squadron, having been slowed by engine
trouble to its lead aircraft, had lagged behind the main
stream.

Elsewhere the Luftwaffe's day ended in rout and
disaster. They'd suffered unsustainable losses – the fighter
pilots of the Eighth Air Force had claimed 161 enemy
fighters destroyed, the highest number ever recorded in a
single day and a feat never to be repeated. It was the last
time that the Luftwaffe put up so many aircraft, and for
such a prolonged battle. For the now crippled Luftwaffe,
the noose had tightened another notch.

103

*Robin Olds, flying his P-51K 'Scat VI',
leads a flight of Mustangs of the 434th
Fighter Squadron, 479th Fighter Group
low over the historic estuary town of
Maldon in Essex. The flight heads home to
their base at Wattisham after an arduous
eight-hour bomber escort mission on
14 February 1945.*

Robert Taylor

DOUBLE ACE DAY

MONDAY 14 FEBRUARY 45
MALDON Essex
479th Fighter Group

Maldon, located on the Blackwater Estuary in Essex, is one of the oldest towns in England. Its quayside had once witnessed Roman trading ships tied alongside the coastal moorings at a time when salt began to be harvested from the sea here. Centuries before Adolf Hitler threatened invasion, the little town had survived assault by previous foreign pillagers, including the Vikings.

In February 1945, with the threat of invasion long gone, the little town was a welcoming sight to the P-51 pilots of the 479th Fighter Group as they headed up the settled waters of the Blackwater Estuary towards their home base at Wattisham.

Monday 14 February was still bitterly cold as the exhausted pilots of the 479th Fighter Group, '*Riddle's Raiders*', skimmed over the top of the ancient English port after an eight-hour round trip to Magdeburg. For the man who commanded the 434th Fighter Squadron it had been a very successful day. With seven victories already under his belt, Major Robin Olds had just notched up another three enemy aircraft that day, bringing his tally to ten, making him a double Ace.

The pilots of the 479th Fighter Group had been escorting B-24 Liberators of the Second Air Division towards their target of Magdeburg, when the call over their headsets came – two Messerschmitt Bf 109s had been spotted in the distance. Major Olds, who was leading Green Section of the 434rd Fighter Squadron, was flying in his usual P-51 Mustang '*Scat IV*'. Olds spotted the danger at once but what he saw now were four fighters, not two. The pilots of Green Section sprang into action behind their aggressive leader.

The formation of Mustangs quickly climbed through the surrounding cirrus in pursuit of the Messerschmitt Bf 109s. Olds closed in on the enemy and squeezed off a couple of solid bursts, immediately striking one of the German aircraft with deadly accuracy, the enemy fighter bursting into flames under the six .50 calibre machine-guns of Olds' Mustang. Just as Olds was closing in he noticed some Focke-Wulf Fw 190s heading towards a formation of B-17s attacking a target near Chemnitz. Above the pursuing Fw 190s was another pair of Messerschmitt Bf 109s providing top cover. Olds rolled out towards the top cover Bf 109s and fired an accurate burst into one of the German fighters. The Bf 109 burst into flames as Olds broke off the attack and turned his attention to the tail of one of the Focke-Wulf Fw 190s that was now bearing down on the American bomber formation. Once again, Olds accurately fired a deadly burst into the Focke-Wulf fighter, destroying it in a matter of seconds. His three victories that day had taken just 30 minutes.

STORMBIRDS RISING | Robert Taylor

Robert Taylor

TOO LITTLE, TOO LATE

History is full of 'what ifs'. What if Harold had turned his head a second earlier during the Battle of Hastings and the Norman arrow had missed his eye? History books may have remembered Harold the Great not William the Conqueror. And what if Gavrilo Princip had aimed a bit too high when shooting at Archduke Ferdinand on the dusty streets of Sarajevo? Two world wars might have been avoided. And 'what if' Hitler had only listened to the views of *General der Jagdflieger* Adolf Galland, his head of Luftwaffe Day Fighter Command, about the tactical use of the revolutionary Messerschmitt Me 262 jet?

From the moment Galland flew an early prototype of Willi Messerschmitt's brilliant new jet aircraft in May 1943, he realised its potential as a fighter; its speed and capabilities far exceeded anything the Allies had to offer. First he requested, then eventually implored the Führer to cease manufacturing the ageing Messerschmitt Bf 109

fighter and immediately switch production to the new jet. Galland was convinced that the Me 262 was the fighter that would reverse the balance of the air campaign, and that this innovative new aircraft was the answer to defeating the ever-growing strength of the Eighth Air Force. Hitler, however, had other plans.

Blinkered by obsession, he decreed that increased production of the new jet should proceed – but as a ground attack fighter-bomber – known as the 'Stormbird'. Far less effort was to be expended on the 'Swallow', the fighter version. By the time Hitler relented, it was far too late.

Only in August 1944, well over a year since Galland's first flight, and several months after its initial deployment with the trials unit *Kommando Novotny*, did small numbers of the new Me 262 fighter finally engage the Eighth Air Force in combat.

The results were immediate. Such was the impact of

the new jet that General Carl Spaatz, former commander of the Eighth Air Force and now in charge of all the U.S. Air Forces in Europe, aired his view 'that if large numbers of these new fighters appeared, they were very likely to inflict such heavy losses on the Eighth's bomber formations that daylight offensive missions might have to be curtailed'.

It was exactly as Galland had predicted. If Hitler had listened to his General, Spaatz's prediction for the Eighth Air Force bombing campaign would have been right. But instead the Luftwaffe's top general was fired; his outspoken views had made him enemies with Hermann Göring, and unpopular with Nazi High Command. Dismissed from his post, Galland now directed his energies into forming Jadgeschwader JV44, his own 'squadron of experts'. Not only was this elite unit equipped with Me 262s, but they were flown by some of the best hand-picked fighter Aces in the Luftwaffe.

CLOSE ENCOUNTERS

Robert Taylor

Eighth Air Force weather forecasters were used to it by now: conditions were once again an operational challenge for the mission planners. Today it wasn't sleet or snow, freezing fog or rain in England that was causing them concern but heavy cloud over eastern Germany.

Throughout March the Eighth Air Force had been in frequent contact with the Me 262s of Jagdgeschwader JG7 'Novotny'. Only the day before, when the Eighth had mounted its biggest assault of the war with some 1,327 bombers hitting targets in advance of the Russian Army, the heavies had run into serious trouble from large formations of menacing German jets. Eight B-17s had been lost in the encounters and the bomber crews were more than wary of what they might expect this time.

Although not quite as large as the mission of the previous day, the Eighth had still managed to get an impressive number of aircraft airborne. Over 1,200 bombers and 675 fighters were being sent to hit airfields and other targets in the east, close to the Czechoslovakian border. Two of the three Bomb Divisions now found themselves hampered by the heavy cloud, forcing them to switch their attacks to secondary targets. The cloud tops, however, gave a large formation of Me 262s from JG7 the perfect camouflage from which to launch their attack.

Concentrating on the B-17s in the Third Division as they began their bomb run on to their targets in Zwickau, 60 miles south-west of Dresden, the Me 262s screamed into the Fortresses with closing speeds almost three times greater than that of the bombers. The jets hit hard and three Fortresses went down in quick succession before the escorts could react. Unfortunately such close encounters were becoming commonplace.

The Me 262 was by far the Luftwaffe's most prolific jet aircraft of World War II. Its gun platform of four 30mm cannon, situated in its nose, made it a deadly adversary for the Eighth Air Force. But it wasn't the Luftwaffe's only jet, or the first. The 'honour' of building the first successful jet aircraft fell to Ernst Heinkel who'd developed the world's first practical turbo-jet engine installed in his experimental Heinkel He178. This single-seat fighter first flew on 27 August 1939 but, even with a series of modifications and improvements, it had failed to impress the German High Command.

Nor was the Me 262 the largest. The Arado 234, a twin-engine jet bomber, entered service in August 1944. The manufacturer, Arado Flugzeugwerke, was best known and associated with seaplanes and trainers. Although the Arado 234 was longer, wider and heavier than the Messerschmitt Me 262, it was far outclassed by the latter's performance.

The final German jet to enter combat, the 'cheap and cheerful' Heinkel He 162 *Volksjäger* – the *People's Jet* – was a single-seat fighter built mainly of wood. It might have been an inexpensive way of getting it ramped into mass production, but the jet was unreliable, and dangerous to fly. Rushed from design to first flight in little over two months it suffered from inadequate testing, a dearth of engine problems, scant facilities and adhesive weaknesses. Designed to be flown by inexperienced pilots, the He 162 *Volksjäger* was afflicted by stability and structural problems right from the start, all as a result of a hasty construction programme. Of the 200 or so built, few saw combat.

COMBAT OVER THE REICH | Robert Taylor

A large force of Me 262 jet fighters from JG7 intercepted a formation of B-17s of the 452nd Bomb Group en route to bomb the oil refinery at Zwickau, 60 miles south of Dresden, 19 March 1945.

DESOLATION AND DESPERATION

TUESDAY 10 APRIL 45
Nr. ORANIENBURG north-west of Berlin
356th Fighter Group

As the war entered its final, bloody climax and the Allies crossed the Rhine, the shattered German Armies fought on regardless, even as the last vestiges of their once-glorious Third Reich were engulfed by scenes of Wagnerian proportions. In the east, vast and vindictive Russian hordes drove mercilessly towards their goal – to conquer and capture the German capital Berlin. Diehard and fanatical Nazis refused to surrender to a fate they

Streaming contrails in the cold, clear air B-17s from the First Air Division come under attack from several Me 262s. But the hunter becomes the hunted as P-51 pilot Wayne Gatlin from the 356th Fighter Group, skilfully positions himself behind the Me 262 ready for the kill.

assumed was final. They would rather fight to the death, while others fled westward to escape capture by the advancing Russian Army.

In the air little of substance remained of the Luftwaffe – at best a bizarre mix of battle-weary fighters and exhausted pilots. Makeshift units hampered by a lack of fuel and ammunition, starved of spare parts, and with few places to hide were the best that the once-mighty Luftwaffe could now produce to defend the skies over Germany. Bridges and forests now sheltered planes from the eyes of prowling Allied fighters, oft-repaired stretches of road doubled as runways, as did the high Alpine meadows in the Nazi mountain strongholds of Bavaria.

On Tuesday 10 April 1945, the Eighth Air Force assembled over 1,200 bombers, protected by all 15 of their Fighter Groups. Among the targets that day were those airfields and facilities suspected of harbouring the Luftwaffe's dwindling arsenal of jets. One of those was at Oranienburg, the factory airfield at which Ernst Heinkel had built his famous Heinkel He111 twin-engine bomber, and where he'd developed the world's first jet engine in the late 1930s. Today the First Division's Fortresses were intending to wipe those facilities off the map.

They succeeded and having released their bombs, turned and headed west for the long journey home. Spirits were high – mission accomplished. Or so they thought.

Unknown to them, a powerful force of nearly fifty Me 262s was already airborne, hidden in high cirrus, waiting for the B-17s on their return.

Inexplicably diving in ones or twos instead of en-masse, they nevertheless pounced on the bomber stream and began picking off the bombers from the rear. Although the Fortress gunners claimed hits, five B-17s were shot down before the escorting P-51s from the 356th Fighter Group could react and drive the attackers

off. Elsewhere five Fortresses in the Third Division met a similar fate but had the Me 262s concentrated their attacks, both Divisions might have been mauled. Eighth Air Force Fighter Command had a very successful day, claiming over 20 aerial victories, several of them being Messerschmitt Me 262s. Low-level strafing was even more profitable – some 335 enemy aircraft destroyed on the ground.

Despite its speed and heavy fire-power, the Me 262s did have one major flaw – their lack of range. With a flight time barely in excess of 30 minutes, the jets were soon forced to break off contact and return to base to re-fuel and re-arm. It didn't take the prowling P-51 fighter pilots long to catch on and hit the jets as they slowed down and prepared to land. The tactic worked – most victories over jets were obtained this way.

SURPRISE ATTACK | Robert Taylor

Whilst attacking a B-17 formation southeast of Berlin on 10 April 1945, Oberleutnant Walter Schuck, flying his Me 262 with JG7, is caught in a surprise attack by the P-51 Mustang of Flt Lt Joseph Peterburs of the 20th Fighter Group.

MUSTANGS ON THE PROWL

MONDAY 16 APRIL 45
Western Bavaria

Shortages of fuel, pilots and spares meant that the Luftwaffe was degraded into making a few desperate appearances in the air. The little that was left was increasingly grounded, for which they paid a heavy price. Seeking out such targets of opportunity, complete groups of P-51s were now sweeping the entire western portion of the Reich, strafing anything hostile they could find, including parked enemy aircraft.

Today, after escorting over 700 heavies to bomb railway marshalling yards, sidings and bridges in eastern Bavaria, fifteen Fighter Groups had gone on a strafing spree attacking 40 airfields in western Czechoslovakia, claiming a record number of 747 aircraft destroyed on the ground. In the same area on the following day they claimed an additional 250 aircraft destroyed in vicious strafing attacks. There wasn't much left for the P-51s to hit and for Germany, with the Führer holed up in his Berlin bunker, time had finally run out.

THE FINAL MISSION

WEDNESDAY 25 APRIL 45
MISSION #968
PILSEN Czechoslovakia

On this day the Eighth flew its final heavy bomber operations of the war, the last of 968 combat missions involving over 523,000 sorties. This final strike at Nazi Germany involved nearly 600 bombers and four Fighter Groups. Whilst the Second Division's B-24s struck out to hit rail yards, a power station and the few airstrips still thought to be operating in south-eastern Germany, the First Division's B-17s headed for the airfield and large Skoda works at Pilsen in western Czechoslovakia. And even on this, its final day of combat, six bombers and a P-51 were sadly lost to the flak guns of an unforgiving enemy.

Lieutenant Hilton O. Thompson, a P-51 pilot with the 479th Fighter Group escorting some of the B-24s near Salzburg, spotted a fast jet, not an Me 262 but an Arado Ar 234 bomber. Managing to surprise the jet from the rear, Thompson unleashed a long volley of fire from his six .50 calibre machine-guns and the Arado fell to the ground. Thompson's victory was the last Luftwaffe aircraft to be shot down by the Eighth Air Force in World War II. It was Thompson's second victory over a jet, a rare feat.

RUNNING THE GAUNTLET | Robert Taylor

Me 262s of JV44 returning to base in southern Germany, having come under attack from P-51 Mustangs of the 353rd Fighter Group. Almost out of fuel and ammunition, the Me 262s have little option but to complete their landing sequence.

As Berlin crumbled around him, Hitler committed suicide on 30 April, two days before the remnants of his capital's garrison surrendered to the Russians. In his will, the Führer bequeathed a distasteful legacy to his named successor, Grand Admiral Karl Dönitz. Over the following hours the Reich imploded as German forces, one by one, began to lay down their arms in surrender.

In the early hours of 7 May 1945, General Alfred Jodl, Chief-of-Staff of German High Command, unconditionally surrendered all German armed forces to the Allies. The unconditional surrender of the Third Reich was confirmed by Field Marshal Wilhelm Keitel in an official signing ceremony the following day in Berlin.

Now, for the Eighth Air Force and the Allies, the war in Europe was finally won. It was all over.

The United States Eighth Air Force was the largest air armada ever assembled in human history and has been rightly regarded as one of the greatest fighting units in the history of warfare.

MUSTANGS ON THE PROWL | Robert Taylor

Lt Colonel Elwyn Righetti, Commanding Officer of the 338th Fighter Squadron, 55th Fighter Group, the 'King of Strafers' with over 20 victories to his credit, leads his P-51 pilots through the Rhine Gorge, skimming the ancient Castle of Stableck, as they seek out enemy targets on their way back to England.

The Eighth Air Force daylight bombing campaign played a major part in the defeat of Germany. In over three years of operations they dropped some 700,000 tons of bombs, inflicting destruction on a scale from which the enemy could never recover. Its fighters, too, had played their part, destroying over 5,200 enemy aircraft in the air and another 4,200 on the ground.

Yet the cost of victory made for sober reading; the six B-17s that went down on the Eighth's final mission were the last of some 6,130 bombers and fighters they had lost during the campaign.

The cost of casualties and the loss of Eighth Air Force airmen were even more sobering. Over 26,000 Eighth Air Force crew members were killed in action. Another 28,000 were taken as prisoners of war.

The courage and sacrifice of those who flew in the 'Mighty Eighth' helped rid the world of one of the worst tyrannies humankind has ever witnessed. The deeds and endeavours of those brave airmen will never be forgotten by future generations for whose peace, liberty and freedom they had fought so valiantly to protect.

AIR SUPERIORITY | Robert Taylor

April 1945, and with the War virtually over, P-51 Mustangs of the 357th Fighter Group sweep unopposed at low level through the beautiful Rhine valley.

'The Americans gave us the best they had, and they gave us everything we needed as and when the need arose. I hope, indeed, I know, that we did everything possible for them in turn.

We could have had no better brothers in arms than Ira Eaker, Fred Anderson and Jimmy Doolittle, and the Americans could have had no better commanders than these three. I was, and am, privileged to count all three of them as the closest of friends.

As for the American bomber crews, they were the bravest of the brave, and I know that I am speaking for my own bomber crews when I pay this tribute.'

Air Chief Marshal Sir Arthur 'Bomber' Harris RAF

COMPANY OF HEROES | Robert Taylor

B-17s of the 34th Bomb Group returning from a raid during the final weeks of the war.

EAGLES OVER THE RHINE | Robert Taylor

The war is over and P-51s of the 353rd Fighter Group make a low-level celebratory run over the ancient town of Kaub, situated on the Rhine south of Remagen.

BOMB GROUPS

Source: The Mighty Eighth by Roger A. Freeman reproduced with kind permission of the Roger Freeman Trust

In the book text 'Bombardment' Groups (BG) are referred as 'Bomb Groups', and the suffix H-Heavy, M-Medium or L-Light etc have been omitted. The respective Bomb Squadrons identified in this chapter are referred and abbreviated to BS.

Stations & dates refer to principle locations and movements only. Air and ground echelons often arrived within days of each other and some units may have been located elsewhere on a temporary basis.

15th BOMBARDMENT SQUADRON (L)

See page 126

25th BOMBARDMENT GROUP (R)

Established Eighth Air Force – 22 Apr 44 as 802nd Reconnaissance Group (P) Re-activated as 25th Bombardment Group (Recon.) on 9 Aug 44.

Squadrons: 652nd (H) / 653rd (L) / 654th (SP) Bomb Squadrons
Combat Aircraft: B-17F (Sep 43 – May 44)
B-17G (from Nov 43)
B-24J (Jul – Nov 44)
Mosquito Mk.XVI (from Apr 44 with 653rd and 654th BS)
B-26G, 654th BS (few)
Stations: WATTON 22 Apr 44 – 23 Jul 45
First Mission: 22 Apr 44

Originally formed for conducting Atlantic meteorological flights and later conducted for reconnaissance and weather scouting operations in enemy air space.

34th BOMBARDMENT GROUP (H)

Assigned Eighth Air Force – Apr 44

Squadrons: 4th / 7th / 18th / 391st Bomb Squadrons (H)
Combat Aircraft: B-24H & J
B-17G (from 17 Sep 44)
Station: MENDELSHAM 18 Apr 44 – 2 Aug 45
First Mission: 23 May 44 Last Mission: 20 Apr 45

The 34th were the oldest USAAF bomb group to serve with Eighth Air Force

44th BOMBARDMENT GROUP (H)

'The Flying Eightballs'
Assigned Eighth Air Force – Sep 42

Squadrons: 66th / 67th / 68th & 506th Bomb Squadrons (H)
(506th assigned from Mar 43)
Combat Aircraft: B-24D, B-24H / J & L
B-24M & B-24M Eagle
Stations: CHEDDINGTON 11 Sep – 9 Oct 42
SHIPDHAM 10 Oct 42 – 15 Jun 45
First Mission: 7 Nov 42 Last Mission: 25 Apr 45

Two Distinguished Unit Citations: 14 May 1943 – Kiel, Germany
1 Aug 1943 – Ploesti, Romania

The first USAAF group to be equipped with Consolidated B-24 Liberators, the 44th BG operated from England for a longer period than any other B-24 group and claimed more enemy fighters destroyed than any other Eighth Air Force B-24 group. Col Leon W. Johnson (Commanding Officer, 4 Jan – 2 Sep 43) was awarded the Medal of Honor for his actions during the Ploesti Raid, Sunday 1 Aug 43.

91st BOMBARDMENT GROUP (H)

'Wray's Ragged lrregulars'
Assigned Eighth Air Force – Sep 42

Squadrons: 322nd / 323rd / 324th & 401st Bomb Squadrons (H)
Combat Aircraft: B-17F & G
Stations: KIMBOLTON 12 Sep – 13 Oct 42
BASSINGBOURN 14 Oct 42 – 23 Jun 45
First Mission: 7 Nov 42 Last Mission: 25 Apr 45

Two Distinguished Unit Citations: 11 Jan 1944 – Oschersleben, Germany
4 Mar 1943 – Hamm, Germany

The 91st Bomb Group led the famous Regensburg / Schweinfurt 'Double Strike' mission of 17 Aug 1943, and was the first Eighth Air Force group to complete 100 missions. However, they also suffered the highest number of losses of all the Eighth Air Force bomber groups.

92nd BOMBARDMENT GROUP (H)

'Fame's Favoured Few'
Assigned Eighth Air Force – Aug 42

Squadrons: 325th / 326th / 327th & 407th Bomb Squadrons (H)
Combat Aircraft: B-17F
B-17 YB-40 'Gunship' (327th BS only)
B-17G
Stations: BOVINGDON 18/28 Aug 42 – 4/11 Jan 43
ALCONBURY 4/11 Jan 43 - 11/15 Sep 43
PODINGTON 11/15 Sep 43 – 20 May / 9 Jul 45
First Mission: 6 Sep – Aug 42 (4 missions)
Acted as Bomber Command Combat Crew Replacement Centre Aug 42 – May 43
Resumed Missions: May 43 Last Mission: 25 Apr 45

Distinguished Unit Citation: 11 Jan 1944 – Oschersleben, Germany

The oldest group in the Eighth Air Force and the first bomb group to fly non-stop across the Atlantic (Aug 42), the 92nd BG fittingly led the last Eighth Air Force mission of the war. The 327th BS was the only unit in the USAAF to be equipped with the YB-40 'Gunship' in combat. Flying Officer (joined RCAF in Aug 41) John C. Morgan, flying with the 326th BS and Co-pilot of B-17F 'Ruthie II', was awarded the Medal of Honor for his actions on 18 Jul 43.

93rd BOMBARDMENT GROUP (H)

'The Travelling Circus'
Assigned Eighth Air Force – 6 Sep 42

Squadrons: 328th / 329th / 330th & 409th Bomb Squadrons (H)
Combat Aircraft: B-24D, B-24H / J / L and B-24M
Stations: ALCONBURY 6 Sep – 6 Dec 42
HARDWICK 6 Dec 42 - 12 Jun 45
First Mission: 9 Oct 42 Last Mission: 25 Apr 45

Two Distinguished Unit Citations: 17 Dec 1942 – 20 Feb 1943 –
Operations in North Africa
1 Aug 1943 – Ploesti, Romania

The oldest B-24 group in the Eighth Air Force, the 93rd Bomb Group flew more missions than any other Eighth Air Force AF Bomb Group.

94th BOMBARDMENT GROUP (H)

Assigned Eighth Air Force – Apr 43

(4 CBW incorporated with 92 CBW in 4th BW(P) from 22 Nov 44 to 16 Feb 45)
Squadrons: 331st / 332nd / 333rd & 410th Bomb Squadrons (H)
Combat Aircraft: B-17F & B-17G
Stations: BASSINGBOURN Mid Apr 43 – 27 May 43
EARLS COLNE 12 May 43 – 12/13 Jun 43
BURY ST EDMUNDS 13 Jun 43 – 12 Dec 45
First Mission: 13 May 43 Last Mission: 21 Apr 45

Two Distinguished Unit Citations: 17 Aug 1943 – Regensburg, Germany
11 Jan 1944 – Brunswick, Germany

95th BOMBARDMENT GROUP (H)

Assigned Eighth Air Force – Apr 43

Squadrons: 334th / 335th / 336th & 412th Bomb Squadrons (H)
Combat Aircraft: B-17F & B-17G
Stations: ALCONBURY 15 Apr – early Jun 43
FRAMLINGHAM 12 May – 15 Jun 43
HORHAM 15 Jun 43 – 3 Aug 45
First Mission: 13 May 43 Last Mission: 20 Apr 45

Three Distinguished Unit Citations: 17 Aug 1943 – Regensburg, Germany
10 Oct 1943 – Munster, Germany
4 Mar 1944 – Berlin, Germany

The only Eighth Air Force group awarded three Distinguished Unit Citations. The 95th BG held the highest total claim of enemy aircraft destroyed. They were the first USAAF group to bomb Berlin, Germany (4 Mar 1944)

96th BOMBARDMENT GROUP (H)

Assigned Eighth Air Force – Apr 43

Squadrons: 337th / 338th / 339th & 413th Bomb Squadrons (H)
Combat Aircraft: B-17F & B-17G
Stations: GRAFTON UNDERWOOD 16 Apr – 27 May 43
ANDREWSFIELD 13 May – 11 Jun 43
SNETTERTON HEATH 12 Jun 43 – c.11 Dec 45
First Mission: 14 May 43 Last Mission: 21 Apr 45

Two Distinguished Unit Citations: 17 Aug 1943 – Regensburg, Germany
9 Apr 1944 – Poznan, Germany

97th BOMBARDMENT GROUP (H)

See page 126

100th BOMBARDMENT GROUP (H)

'The Bloody Hundredth'

Assigned Eighth Air Force – Jun 43

Squadrons: 349th / 350th / 351st & 418th Bomb Squadrons (H)
Combat Aircraft: B-17F & B-17G
Stations: PODINGTON   2 Jun – 8 Jun 43
               THORPE ABBOTTS   9 Jun 43 – c.11 Dec 45
First Mission: 25 Jun 43   Last Mission: 20 Apr 45

Two Distinguished Unit Citations: *17 Aug 1943 – Regensburg, Germany*
                                           3, 4, 6 Mar 1944 – Berlin, Germany

301st BOMBARDMENT GROUP (H)

See page 126

303rd BOMBARDMENT GROUP (H)

'Hell's Angels'

Assigned Eighth Air Force – 10 Sep 42

Squadrons: 358th / 359th / 360th & 427th Bomb Squadrons (H)
Combat Aircraft: B-17F & B-17G
Station: MOLESWORTH   12 Sep 42 – 11 Jun 45
First Mission: 17 Nov 42   Last Mission: 25 Apr 45

Distinguished Unit Citations: 11 Jan 1944 – Oschersleben, Germany

The 303rd Bomb Group was the first Eighth Air Force Bomb Group to complete 300 missions and flew more missions than any other Eighth Air Force B-17 Bomb Group (364 missions). Two members of the 303rd BG were awarded the Medal of Honor: Lt Jack W. Mathis (18 Mar 43) and T/Sgt Forrest L. Vosler (20 Dec 43).

Three famous B-17s flew with the group:
B-17F 'Hell's Angels'- the first B-17 to complete 25 missions
B-17F 'Knock-Out Dropper' – the first B-17 to complete 50 and 75 missions
B-17G 'Thunderbird' – one of the few B-17s to fly more than 100 missions

305th BOMBARDMENT GROUP (H)

'Can Do'

Assigned Eighth Air Force – Sep 42

Squadrons: 364th / 365th / 366th & 422nd Bomb Squadrons (H)
Combat Aircraft: B-17F & B-17G
Stations: GRAFTON UNDERWOOD   12 Sep – 11 Dec 42
                CHELVESTON   6/11 Dec 42 – 25 Jul 45
First Mission: 17 Nov 42   Last Mission: 25 Apr 45

Two Distinguished Unit Citations: *11 Jan 1944 – Oschersleben, Germany*
                                           4 Apr 1943 – Paris, France

Under the command of Colonel Curtis E. LeMay (Commanding Officer 04 Jun 42 – 15 May 43), the 305th Bomb Group pioneered many of the formation and bombing procedures that became standard tactics for Eighth Air Force Bomber Command. Two members of the 305th Bomb Group were awarded Medals of Honour: First Lieutenant William R. Lawley Jr. (20 Feb 1944), and First Lieutenant Edward S. Michael (11 Apr 1944).

306th BOMBARDMENT GROUP (H)

'The Reich Wreckers'

Assigned Eighth Air Force – Sep 42

Squadrons: 367th / 368th / 369th & 423rd Bomb Squadrons (H)
Combat Aircraft: B-17F & B-17G
Station: THURLEIGH   7 Sep 42 – 15 Dec 45
First Mission: 9 Oct 42   Last Mission: 19 Apr 45

Two Distinguished Unit Citations: *11 Jan 1944 – Oschersleben, Germany*
                                           22 Feb 1944 – Bernburg, Germany

The 306th Bomb Group was the oldest operational bomb group in the Eighth Air Force and was stationed in England, and at one airbase, longer than any other group. First group over Germany, 27 Jan 1943 – target: Wilhelmshaven. Ball-Turret Gunner, Sgt. Maynard H. Smith was awarded the Medal of Honor on his first mission – 1 May 43.

322nd BOMBARDMENT GROUP (M)

Assigned Eighth Air Force – 12 Dec 42
Re-assigned Ninth Air Force – 16 Oct 43

Squadrons: 449th / 450th / 451st & 452nd Bomb Squadrons (M)
Combat Aircraft: B-26B & C Marauder
Stations: BURY ST. EDMUNDS   1 Dec 42 – 12 Jun 43
                RATTLESDEN   Dec 42 – Apr 43
                                   (451st & 452nd gnd. esc. only)
                ANDREWSFIELD   12 Jun 43 – 19 Sep 44
First Mission: 14 May 43   Last Mission with Eighth Air Force:
                                   8 Oct 43

First group to operate the Martin B-26 Marauder from the UK – 14 May 43

SKIPPER COMES HOME | Robert Taylor

'Skipper' – one of the longest serving B-17 Fortresses of the war – and other B-17's of the 367th Squadron, 306th Bomb Group, return to base at Thurleigh in East Anglia, late January 1945.

Keith Burns

323rd BOMBARDMENT GROUP (M)

Assigned Eighth Air Force – 12 May 43
Reassigned to Ninth Air Force – 16 Oct 43

Squadrons:	453rd / 454th / 455th & 456th Bomb Squadrons (M)	
Combat Aircraft:	B-26B & B-26C Marauder	
Stations:	HORHAM	21 May – 14 Jun 43
	EARLS COLNE	14 Jun 43 – 11/27 Jul 44
First Mission:	16 Jul 43	Last Mission with Eighth Air Force: 9 Oct 43

351st BOMBARDMENT GROUP (H)

Assigned Eighth Air Force – Apr 43

Squadrons:	508th / 509th / 510th & 511th Bomb Squadrons (H)	
Combat Aircraft:	B-17F & B-17G	
Station:	POLEBROOK	15 Apr 43 – 23 Jun 45
First Mission:	14 May 43	Last Mission: 20 Apr 45

Two Distinguished Unit Citations: 9 Oct 1943 – Anklam, Germany
                                          11 Jan 1944 – Oschersleben, Germany

379th BOMBARDMENT GROUP (H)

Assigned Eighth Air Force – Apr 43

Squadrons:	524th / 525th / 526th & 527th Bomb Squadrons (H)	
Combat Aircraft:	B-17 F & B-17G	
Stations:	KIMBOLTON	20 May 43 – 12 Jun 45
First Mission:	29 May 43	Last Mission: 25 Apr 45

The 379th Bomb Group flew more sorties than any other Eighth Air Force Bomb Group and dropped a greater bomb tonnage than any other group. The 379th Bomb Group B-17G 'Ol Gappy' flew 157 missions, probably more than any other in the Eighth Air Force. Awarded the 'Grand Slam' in April 1944 for best bombing accuracy, greatest tonnage, greatest number of aircraft attacking with the lowest losses and abortive rate.

381st BOMBARDMENT GROUP (H)

Assigned Eighth Air Force – May 43

Squadrons:	532nd / 533rd / 534th & 535th Bomb Squadrons (H)	
Combat Aircraft:	B-17F & B-17G	
Station:	RIDGEWELL	31 Jun 43 – 24 Jun 45
First Mission:	22 Jun 43	Last Mission: 25 Apr 45

The 381st Bomb Group suffered the heaviest losses of all the groups that participated on the Regensburg / Schweinfurt 'Double Strike' mission – 17 Aug 43.

384th BOMBARDMENT GROUP (H)

Assigned Eighth Air Force – May 43

Squadrons:	544th / 545th / 546th & 547th Bomb Squadrons (H)	
Combat Aircraft:	B-17F & B-17G	
Station:	GRAFTON UNDERWOOD	25 May 43 – 16 Jun 45
First Mission:	22 Jun 43	Last Mission: 25 Apr 45

Two Distinguished Unit Citations: 11 Jan 1944 – Oschersleben, Germany
                                          24 Apr 1944 – Oberpfaffenhofen, Germany

On 25 Apr 1945 the 384th Bomb Group dropped the last Eighth Air Force bombs of the war.

385th BOMBARDMENT GROUP (H)

'Van's Valiants'
Assigned Eighth Air Force – Jun 43

Squadrons:	548th / 549th / 550th & 551st Bomb Squadrons (H)	
Combat Aircraft:	B-17F & B-17G	
Station:	GREAT ASHFIELD	26 Jun 43 – 4 Aug 45
First Mission:	17 Jul 43	Last Mission: 20 Apr 45

Two Distinguished Unit Citations: 17 Aug 1943 – Regensburg, Germany
                                          12 May 1944 – Zwickau, Germany

The 385th Bomb Group led the famous attack on Marienburg, Germany – 9 Oct 1943 and, in May 1945, had the distinction of being the last group to be shot at by enemy anti-aircraft over Holland.

386th BOMBARDMENT GROUP (M)

Assigned Eighth Air Force – 4 Jun 43
Re-assigned to the Ninth Air Force – 15 Oct 43

Squadrons:	552nd / 553rd / 554th & 555th Bomb Squadrons (M)	
Combat Aircraft:	B-26F & B-26C Marauder	
Stations:	SNETTERTON HEATH	3 Jun – 10 Jun 43
	BOXTED	10 Jun – 24 Sep 43
	GREAT DUNMOW	24 Sep 43 – 2 Oct 44
First Mission:	30 Jul 43	Last Mission with the Eighth Air Force: 8 Oct 43

Distinguished Unit Citation: 30 Jul 1943 – 30 Jul 1944 – Operations during the period. The 386th Bomb Group was re-assigned for tactical operations in France in Oct 1944 in support of the Allied advance in Europe.

387th BOMBARDMENT GROUP (M)

Assigned Eighth Air Force – 25 Jun – 16 Oct 43
Re-assigned to the Ninth Air Force – 16 Oct 43

Squadrons:	556th / 557th / 558th & 559th Bomb Squadrons (M)	
Combat Aircraft:	B-26B & B-26C Marauder	
Station:	CHIPPING ONGAR	21 Jun 43 – 18 Jul 44
First Mission:	15 Aug 43	Last Mission with the Eighth Air Force: 9 Oct 43

The 387th Bomb Group was re-assigned for tactical operations in France in Oct 1944 in support of the Allied advance in Europe.

HELPING HAND | Robert Taylor

Lucky to have found support from a long-range Mustang who now rides 'shotgun', a damaged B-17 struggles safely home to base.

398th BOMBARDMENT GROUP (H)

Assigned Eighth Air Force – Apr 44

Squadrons:	600th / 601st / 602nd & 603rd Bomb Squadrons (H)	
Combat Aircraft:	B-17G	
Station:	NUTHAMPSTEAD	22 Apr 44 – 22 Jun 45
First Mission:	6 May 44	Last Mission: 25 Apr 45

401st BOMBARDMENT GROUP (H)

Assigned Eighth Air Force – Nov 43

Squadrons:	612th / 613th / 614th & 615th Bomb Squadrons (H)	
Combat Aircraft:	B-17G	
Station:	DEENETHORPE	3 Nov 43 – 20 Jun 45
First Mission:	26 Nov 43	Last Mission: 20 Apr 45

The 401st Bomb Group achieved the second best rating in bombing accuracy in the Eighth Air Force.

445th BOMBARDMENT GROUP (H)

Assigned Eighth Air Force – Nov 43

Squadrons:	700th / 701st / 702nd & 703rd Bomb Squadrons (H)	
Combat Aircraft:	B-24H / J / L & M	
Station:	TIBENHAM	4 Nov 43 – 28 May 45
First Mission:	13 Dec 43	Last Mission: 25 Apr 45

On 27 Sep 44, the 445th Bomb Group suffered the highest Group loss on a single mission (Kassel, Germany) in one campaign when 28 out of 35 B-24 Liberators were lost.

446th BOMBARDMENR GROUP (H)

'Bungay Buckeroos'

Assigned Eighth Air Force – Nov 43

Squadrons:	704th / 705th / 706th & 707th Bomb Squadrons (H)	
Combat Aircraft:	B-24H / J / L & M	
Station:	BUNGAY	4 Nov 43 – 5 Jul 45
First Mission:	16 Dec 43	Last Mission: 25 Apr 45

B-24H 'Ronnie' from the 446th Bomb Group's 704th BS is believed to be the first Eighth Air Force Liberator to complete 100 missions. The 706th BS flew 62 consecutive missions, and the 707th BS flew 68 consecutive missions, without loss.

388th BOMBARDMENT GROUP (H)

Assigned Eighth Air Force – Jun 43

Squadrons:	560th / 561st / 562nd & 563rd Bomb Squadrons (H)	
Combat Aircraft:	B-17F & B-17G	
	B-24 'Aphrodite'	
Station:	KNETTISHALL	23 Jun 43 – c.5 Aug 45
	FERSFIELD (Aphrodite Project)	12 Jul 44 – 1 Jan 45
First Mission:	17 Jul 43	Last Mission: Apr 45

Participated in Operation 'Aphrodite', the use of radio-controlled heavy bombers packed with high explosives, as guided-missile drones.

389th BOMBARDMENT GROUP (H)

'The Sky Scorpions'

Assigned Eighth Air Force – 11 Jun 43

Squadrons:	564th / 565th / 566th & 567th Bomb Squadrons (H)	
Combat Aircraft:	B-24D / H / J / L & M	
Station:	HETHEL	11 Jun 43 – 30 May 45
First Mission:	9 Jul 43 (first from UK: 7 Sep 43)	Last Mission: 25 Apr 45

The 389th was one of the three Eighth Air Force B-24 Groups that took part in the 1 Aug 43 Ploesti Raid. Second Lieutenant Lloyd H. Hughes was posthumously awarded the Medal of Honor – 1 Aug 43. The Group's 564th Bomb Squadron was judged on efficiency 'the best squadron in the ETO in 1945'.

390th BOMBARDMENT GROUP (H)

'Wittan's Wallopers'

Assigned Eighth Air Force – Jul 43

Squadrons:	568th / 569th / 570th & 571st Bomb Squadrons (H)	
Combat Aircraft:	B-17F & B-17G	
Station:	FRAMLINGHAM	14 Jul 43 – 4 Aug 45
First Mission:	12 Aug 43	Last Mission: 20 Apr 45
Two Distinguished Unit Citations:	17 Aug 1943 – Ploesti, Romania	
	14 Oct 1943 – Schweinfurt, Germany	

During the mission to Munster, Germany on 10 Oct 1943, the 390th Bomb Group claimed the highest number of enemy aircraft destroyed in a single mission. 390th BG veteran, Sgt. Hewitt 'Buck' Dunn, was the only airman to fly 100 combat missions (104 total missions) with the Eighth Air Force.

392nd BOMBARDMENT GROUP (H)

Assigned Eighth Air Force – Jul 43

Squadrons:	576th / 577th / 578th & 579th Bomb Squadrons (H)	
Combat Aircraft:	B-24H / J / L & M	
Station:	WENDLING	1 Aug 43 – 15 Jun 45
First Mission:	9 Sep 43	Last Mission: 25 Apr 45

Distinguished Unit Citation: 24 Feb 1944 – Gotha, Germany

447th BOMBARDMENT GROUP (H)

Assigned Eighth Air Force – Nov 43

Squadrons:	708th / 709th / 710th & 711th Bomb Squadrons (H)
Combat Aircraft:	B-17G
Station:	RATTLESDEN 30 Nov 43 – 2 Aug 45
First Mission:	24 Dec 43 Last Mission: 21 Apr 45

Second Lieutenant Robert E. Femoyer was posthumously awarded the Medal of Honor for his actions on a raid to Merseburg/Leuna on 2 Nov 44. 447th Bomb Group B-17G 'Milk Wagon' flew 129 missions with no turn-backs.

448th BOMBARDMENT GROUP (H)

Assigned Eighth Air Force – Nov 43

Squadrons:	712th / 713th / 714th & 7l5th Bomb Squadrons (H)
Combat Aircraft:	B-24H / J / L & M
Station:	SEETHING 30 Nov 43 – 6 Jul 45
First Mission:	22 Dec 43 Last Mission: 25 Apr 45

452nd BOMBARDMENT GROUP (H)

Assigned Eighth Air Force – Jan 44

Squadrons:	728th / 729th / 730th & 731st Bomb Squadrons (H)
Combat Aircraft:	B-17G
Station:	DEOPHAM GREEN 3 Jan 44 – 5 Aug 45
First Mission:	5 Feb 44 Last Mission: 21 Apr 45

Distinguished Unit Citation: 7 Apr 1945 – Kaltenkirchen, Germany

First Lieutenant Donald J. Gott (Pilot) and Second Lieutenant William E. Metzger (Co-pilot) were both awarded Medals of Honor whilst flying B-17G 'Lady Janet' with the 729th Bomb Squadron on 9 Nov 44.

453rd BOMBARDMENT GROUP (H)

Assigned Eighth Air Force – Dec 43

Squadrons:	732nd / 733rd / 734th & 735th Bomb Squadrons (H)
Combat Aircraft:	B -24H / J / L & M
Station:	OLD BUCKENHAM 22 Dec 43 – 9 May 45
First Mission:	5 Feb 44 Last Mission: 12 Apr 45

The 733rd Bomb Squadron completed 82 consecutive missions without loss – an Eighth Air Force record. Hollywood film star, James M. Stewart was assigned as Group Executive Officer in Mar 1944.

457th BOMBARDMENT GROUP (H)

Assigned Eighth Air Force – Jan 44

Squadrons:	748th / 749th / 750th & 751st Bomb Squadrons (H)
Combat Aircraft:	B-17G
Station:	GLATTON 21 Jan 44 – 21 Jun 45
First Mission:	21 Feb 44 Last Mission: 20 Apr 45

458th BOMBARDMENT GROUP (H)

Assigned Eighth Air Force – Jan 44

Squadrons:	752nd / 753rd / 754th & 755th Bomb Squadrons (H)
Combat Aircraft:	B-24H / J / L / M
Station:	HORSHAM ST. FAITH 29 Jan 44 – 3 Jul 45
First Mission:	24 Feb 44 Last Mission: 25 Apr 45

466th BOMBARDMENT GROUP (H)

'The Flying Deck'

Assigned Eighth Air Force – Mar 44

Squadrons:	784th / 785th / 786th & 787th Bomb Squadrons (H)
Combat Aircraft:	B-24H / J / L & M
Station:	ATTLEBRIDGE 7 Mar 44 – 6 Jul 45
First Mission:	22 Mar 44 Last Mission: 25 Apr 45

467th BOMBARDMENT GROUP (H)

'The Rackheath Aggies'

Assigned Eighth Air Force – 11 Mar 44

Squadrons:	788th / 789th / 790th & 791st Bomb Squadrons (H)
Combat Aircraft:	B-24
Station:	RACKHEATH 12 Mar 44 – 5 Jul 45
First Mission:	10 Apr 44 Last Mission: 12 Jun 45

The 467th Bomb Group achieved the best overall bombing accuracy in Eighth Air Force Bomber Command. Colonel Albert J. Shower was the only Group Commander in the Eighth Air Force to bring a unit to England and remain in command until the end of hostilities. 467th Bomb Group B-24 'Witchcraft' flew 130 combat missions without an abort, thanks mostly in part to her skilled crew chief, Sgt. Joe Ramirez.

482nd (Pathfinder) BOMBARDMENT GROUP (P)

Assigned Eighth Air Force – 20 Aug 43
Re-assigned to Eighth Air Force Composite Command – Feb 44

Squadrons:	812th / 813th & 814th Bomb Squadrons (P)
Combat Aircraft:	812th B-17F & G H2X, B-17G Eagle
	813th B-17F H2S and Oboe, B-17-G H2X
	814th B-24H and J H2X, B-24L, APS – 15A and B-24 Eagle
Station:	ALCONBURY 20 Aug 43 – 24 Jun 45
First Mission:	27 Sep 43 Last Mission: 27 Mar 45

Distinguished Unit Citation: 11 Jan 1944.
Pioneered radar bombing for the USAAF. Dropped the first Eighth Air Force bombs on the German capital Berlin on 4 Mar 1944 – William Owen crew.

486th BOMBARDMENT GROUP (H)

Assigned Eighth Air Force – Mar 44

Squadrons:	832nd / 833rd & 834th & 835th Bomb Squadrons (H)
Combat Aircraft:	B-24H (Mar 44 – Jul 44)
	B-17G (from Aug 44)
Station:	SUDBURY 5 Apr 44 – 25 Aug 45
First Mission:	7 May 44 Last Mission: 21 Apr 45

487th BOMBARDMENT GROUP (H)

Assigned Eighth Air Force – Apr 44

Squadrons:	836th / 837th / 838th & 839th Bomb Squadrons (H)
Combat Aircraft:	B-24 (Apr 44 – 19 Jul 44)
	B-17 (from 1 Aug 44)
Station:	LAVENHAM 4 Apr 44 – Aug 45
First Mission:	7 May 44 Last Mission: 21 Apr 45

The 487th Bomb Group led the largest Eighth Air Force mission of the war on 24 Dec 1944. General Frederick Castle was killed in action on the same day and posthumously awarded the Medal of Honor.

489th BOMBARDMENT GROUP (H)

Assigned Eighth Air Force – Apr 44 – 29 Nov 44
Redeployed to the USA – 29 Nov 44

Squadrons:	844th / 845th / 846th & 847th Bomb Squadrons (H)
Combat Aircraft:	B-24H & B-24J
Station:	HALESWORTH 22 Apr – 29 Nov 44
First Mission:	30 May 44 Last Mission: 10 Nov 44

On 5 Jun 1944, Lt. Col Leon R. Vance was awarded the only Medal of Honor given to a B-24 crewman for an action flown from England. The 489th Bomb Group was the first Eighth Air Force Bomb Group redeployed to the USA in preparation for Pacific duties, but hostilities ceased before further redeployment.

490th BOMBARDMENT GROUP (H)

Assigned Eighth Air Force – Apr 44

Squadrons:	848th / 849th / 850th & 851st Bomb Squadrons (H)
	(850th BS to 801st BG (P) May 44 then 490th BG Aug 44)
Combat Aircraft:	B-24H & J to 6 Aug 44
	B-17G in combat from 27 Aug 44
Station:	EYE 26 Apr 44 – 24 Aug 45
First Mission:	31 May 44 Last Mission: 20 Apr 45

491st BOMBARDMENT GROUP (H)

'The Ringmasters'

Assigned Eighth Air Force – 1 Jan 44

Squadrons:	852nd / 853rd / 854th & 855th Bomb Squadrons (H)
Combat Aircraft:	B-24H & J, B-24L & M
Stations:	METFIELD 25 Apr – 15 Aug 44
	NORTH PICKENHAM 15 Aug 44 – 4 Jul 45
First Mission:	2 Jun 44 Last Mission: 25 Apr 45

Distinguished Unit Citation: 26 Nov 1944 – Misberg, Germany

The 'Ringmasters' had the highest rate of operations of all B -24 groups.

492nd BOMB GROUP (H)

Assigned Eighth Air Force – Apr 44

Squadrons:	856th / 857th / 858th / & 859th Bomb Squadrons (H)
Combat Aircraft:	B-24H & J
Station:	NORTH PICKENHAM 14 Apr – 12 Aug 44
First Mission:	11 May 44 Last Mission: 7 Aug 44

Re-organised as SPECIAL OPERATIONS GROUP (Aug 44 - see p126)

493rd BOMBARDMENT GROUP (H)

'Helton's Hellcats'

Assigned Eighth Air Force – 1 Jan 44

Squadrons:	860th / 861st / 862nd & 863rd Bomb Squadrons (H)
	(862nd established as Third Scouting Force – 1 Feb 45, to 493rd BG May 45)
Combat Aircraft:	B-24H & J (to 24 Aug 44)
	B-17G (in combat from 8 Sep 44)
Station:	DEBACH 17 Apr 44 – 6 Aug 45
	LITTLE WALDEN 1 Mar 45 – 1 Apr 45 (Air echelon only)
First Mission:	6 Jun 44 Last Mission: 20 Apr 45

The last Eighth Air Force Bomb Group to become operational. Colonel Robert B. Landry (Commanding Officer 16 Feb – May 45) was the only man to command both Fighter and Bomber groups in the Eighth Air Force (56th Fighter Group & 493rd Bomb Group).

AMERICAN EAGLES | Robert Taylor

One of World War Two's best known P-51s, Glamorous Glen III, flown by one of the aviation's best known pilots, Chuck Yeager, together with pilots of the 357th Fighter Group head out of Leiston in Suffolk on an escort mission to Germany in October 1944.

THE MIGHTY EIGHTH
FIGHTER GROUPS

1st FIGHTER GROUP
See page 126

4th FIGHTER GROUP
'The Debden Eagles'
Assigned to the Eighth Air Force – 12 Sep 42 and formed from the three RAF Eagle Squadrons (71, 121 & 133 Squadrons RAF)

Squadrons:	334th / 335th / 336th Fighter Squadrons
Combat aircraft:	Spitfire Mk.V (Sep 42 – Apr 43)
	P-47C (Mar 43 – Feb 44)
	P-47D (Jan 43 – Feb 44)
	P-51B (from Feb 44), P-51D (from Jun 44),
	P-51K (from Dec 44)

Stations:	DEBDEN	29 Sept 42 – 20/27 Jul 45
	STEEPLE MORDEN	20/27 Jul 45 – 4 Nov 45
First Mission:	2 Oct 42	Last Mission: 25 Apr 45

Distinguished Unit Citation: Combat actions between 5 Mar & 24 Apr 1944 – 189 enemy aircraft destroyed as aerial claims / 134 enemy aircraft destroyed as ground claims.

The Fourth Fighter Group was the oldest group in Eighth Air Force Fighter Command and achieved the highest combined victories - 583½ air & 469 ground. They were the first 8th Fighter Group to engage enemy aircraft over both Paris and Berlin and, on 28 Jul 43, the first to penetrate German airspace.

14th FIGHTER GROUP
See page 126

20th FIGHTER GROUP
'The Loco Busters'
Assigned to the Eighth Air Force – 25 Aug 43

Squadrons:	55th / 77th / 79th Fighter Squadrons
Combat aircraft:	P-38 (Aug 43 – Jul 44)
	P-51C & D (from Jul 44), P-51K (from Dec 44)

Stations:	KINGS CLIFFE	26 Aug 43 – 11 Oct 45
First Mission:	28 Dec 43	Last Mission: 25 Apr 45

Distinguished Unit Citation: 8 Apr 44 – Sweep over Germany.

31st FIGHTER GROUP
See page 126

52nd FIGHTER GROUP
See page 126

55th FIGHTER GROUP

Assigned to the Eighth Air Force – 16 Sep 43

Squadrons:	38th / 338th with 3rd Scouting Force / 343rd Fighter Squadrons
Combat aircraft:	P-38 (Sep 43 – Jul 44)
	P-51D (from Jul 44, P-51K (from Dec 44)

Stations:	NUTHAMPSTEAD	16 Sep 43 – 16 Apr 44
	WORMINGTON	16 Apr 44 – 21 Jul 45
First Mission:	15 Oct 43	Last Mission: 21 Apr 45

The 55th Fighter Group were the first to operate the Lockheed P-38 Lightning in combat with Eighth Air Force Fighter Command and the first to penetrate Berlin airspace (3 Mar 44). They destroyed more locos by strafing than any other group. Lt Colonel Elwyn G. Righetti was the top Eighth Air Force strafing pilot.

56th FIGHTER GROUP

'Zemke's Wolfpack'

Assigned to the Eighth Air Force – 12 Jan 43

Squadrons:	61st / 62nd / 63rd Fighter Squadrons
Combat aircraft:	P-47C (Feb 43 – Apr 43)
	P-47D (Jun 43 – Mar 45)
	P-47M (from Jan 45)

Stations:	KINGS CLIFFE	13 Jan – 5 Apr 43
	HORSHAM ST FAITH	5 Apr – 8 Jul 43
	HALESWORTH	8 Jul 43 – 18 Apr 44
	BOXTED	18 Apr 44 – 9 Sep 45
First Mission:	13 Apr 43	Last Mission: 21 Apr 45

Two Distinguished Unit Citations: Combat actions between 20 Feb & 9 Mar 1944 – 98 enemy aircraft destroyed as aerial claims. 18 Sep 1944 – Holland – In support of 'Operation Market Garden'.

The 56th Fighter Group destroyed more enemy aircraft and had more fighter Aces than any other group in Eighth Air Force Fighter Command. They were the first USAAF group to fly the P-47 and the only Eighth Air Force Fighter Group to fly the P-47 throughout the war.

78th FIGHTER GROUP

'The Duxford Eagles'

Assigned to the Eighth Air Force – 29 Nov 42

Squadrons:	82nd / 83rd / 84th Fighter Squadrons
Combat aircraft:	P-38 (Dec 42 – Feb 43)
	P-47C (from Jan 43)
	P-47D (from Jun 43 – Jan 45)
	P-51 & K (from Dec 44)

Stations:	GOXHILL	1 Dec 42 – 3 Apr 43
	DUXFORD	3 Apr 43 – 10 Oct 45
First Mission:	13 Apr 43	Last Mission: 25 Apr 45

Two Distinguished Unit Citations: 16 – 23 Sep 44 – Holland – In support of 'Operation Market Garden'. 16 Apr 45 – Czechoslovakia – Ground strafing.

Capt. Charles P. London was the first Eighth Air Force Ace. The 78th Fighter Group was the only Eighth Air Force Group to fly all three main fighter types: P-38, P-47 & P-51. On 28 Aug 44 two of their pilots, flying P-47s, brought down the first Me 262 jet.

82nd FIGHTER GROUP

See page 126

339th FIGHTER GROUP

Assigned to the Eighth Air Force – 4 Apr 44

Squadrons:	503rd / 504th / 505th Fighter Squadrons
Combat aircraft:	P-51B / P-51C / P-51D & K

Station:	FOWLMERE	5 Apr 44 – 10 Oct 45
First Mission:	30 Apr 44	Last Mission: 21 Apr 45

Distinguished Unit Citation: 10 – 11 Sep 44 – Destruction of 58 enemy aircraft

The 339th Fighter Group had the highest number of combined air & ground victories in a one year period and were the only group to claim over 100 ground strafing victories on two occasions – 105 enemy aircraft destroyed on 4 Apr 45 and 118 enemy aircraft destroyed on 16 Apr 45.

350th FIGHTER GROUP

See page 126

352nd FIGHTER GROUP

'The Blue-nosed Bastards of Bodney'

Assigned to the Eighth Air Force – 6 Jul 43

Squadrons:	328th / 486th / 487th Fighter Squadrons
Combat aircraft:	P-47D (Jul 43 – Apr 44)
	P-51B (from Apr 44), P-51C, P-51D & K

Stations:	BODNEY	8 Jul 43 – 7 Feb 45
	ASCHE	23 Dec 44 – 27 Jan 45 (air ech only)
	CHIEVRES	27 Jan – 13 Apr 45
	BODNEY	13 Apr – 3 Nov 4
First Mission:	9 Sep 43	Last Mission: 3 May 45

Two Distinguished Unit Citations:	8 May 44 – Brunswick, Germany.
	1 Jan 45 – 487th Fighter Squadron – 23 enemy aircraft destroyed.

One of the group's pilots – Major George E. Preddy, was the highest-scoring P-51 Mustang Ace in the Eighth Air Force. On 2 Nov 44 the group destroyed the second highest victory tally in a single day.

353rd FIGHTER GROUP

'The Slybird Group'

Assigned to the Eighth Air Force – 7 Jun 43

Squadrons:	350th / 351st / 352nd Fighter Squadrons
Combat aircraft:	P-47D (Jul 43 – Nov 44)
	P-51D (from Oct 44)
	P-51K (from Dec 44)

Stations:	GOXHILL	7 Jun 43 – 3 Aug 43
	METFIELD	3 Aug 43 – 12 Apr 44
	RAYDON	12 Apr 44 – 10 Oct 45
First Mission:	12 Aug 43	Last Mission: 25 Apr 45

Distinguished Unit Citation: 17 – 23 Sep 44 – Holland – In support of 'Operation Market Garden'.

The 353rd Fighter Group pioneered the P-47 in a dive-bombing and ground attack adaptation which was adopted by both Eighth and Ninth Air Force Fighter Commands.

355th FIGHTER GROUP

'The Steeple Morden Strafers'

Assigned to the Eighth Air Force – 6 Jul 43

Squadrons:	354th with 2nd Scouting Force / 357th / 358th Fighter Squadrons
Combat aircraft:	P-47D (Jul 43 – Mar 44)
	P-51B (from Mar 44)
	P-51D & K

Station:	STEEPLE MORDEN	8 Jul 43 – 3 Jul 45
First Mission:	14 Sep 43	Last Mission: 25 Apr 45

Distinguished Unit Citation: 5 Apr 45 – Attack on airfields in the Munich area.

The 355th fighter Group destroyed more enemy aircraft by strafing than any other group in Eighth Air Force Fighter Command.

356th FIGHTER GROUP

Assigned to the Eighth Air Force – 25 Aug 43

Squadrons:	359th / 360th / 361st Fighter Squadrons
Combat aircraft:	P-47D (Sep 43 – Nov 44)
	P-51D (from Nov 44)
	P-51K (from Dec 44)

Stations:	GOXHILL	27 Aug – 5 Oct 43
	MARTLESHAM HEATH	5 Oct 43 – Nov 45
First Mission:	15 Oct 43	Last Mission: 7 May 45

Distinguished Unit Citation: 17 – 23 Sep 44 – Holland – In support of 'Operation Market Garden'.

The 356th Fighter Group suffered the highest ratio of losses to enemy aircraft than any other group in Eighth Air Force Fighter Group.

357th FIGHTER GROUP

'The Yoxford Boys'

Assigned to the Eighth Air Force – 31 Jan 44

Squadrons:	362nd / 363rd / 364th Fighter Squadrons
Combat aircraft:	P-51B / P-51C / P-51D & K

Stations:	RAYDON	30 Nov 43 – 31 Jan 44
	LEISTON	31 Jan – 8 Jul 45
First Mission:	11 Feb 44	Last Mission: 25 Apr 45

Two Distinguished Unit Citations:	6 Mar & 29 Jun 44 – Escort duties
	14 Jan 45 – Action over Derben, Germany

The first group in the Eighth Air Force to go operational with the P-51 Mustang. The 357th Fighter Group held the record for the highest number of enemy aircraft destroyed in the air on a single mission – 14 Jan 45 – 56 enemy aircraft destroyed.

359th FIGHTER GROUP

Assigned to the Eighth Air Force – 19 Oct 43

Squadrons:	368th / 369th / 370th Fighter Squadrons
Combat aircraft:	P-47D (Nov 43 – May 44)
	P-51B, P-51C (from 5 May 44) P-51D & K

Stations:	EAST WRETHAM	10 Oct 43 – 2 Nov 45
First Mission:	13 Dec 43	Last Mission: 20 Apr 45

Distinguished Unit Citation: 11 Sep 44 – Merseberg, Germany

361st FIGHTER GROUP

'The Yellow Jackets'

Assigned to the eighth Air Force – 30 Nov 43

Squadrons:	374th / 375th / 376th Fighter Squadrons
Combat aircraft:	P-47D (Dec 43 – May 44)
	P-51B, P-51C (from 12 May 44), P-51D & K
Stations:	BOTTISHAM 30 Nov 43 – 26 Sep 44
	LITTLE WALDEN 26 Sep 44 – 4 Feb 45
	ST DIZIER 25 Dec 44 – 15 Feb 45
	CHIEVRES 15 Feb 45 – 9 Apr 45
	LITTLE WRETHAM 9 Apr – 3 Nov 45
First Mission:	21 Jan 44 Last Mission: 20 Apr 45

The last P-47 Thunderbolt Fighter Group to join Eighth Air Force Fighter Command

364th FIGHTER GROUP

Assigned to the Eighth Air Force – 10 Feb 44

Squadrons:	383rd / 384th / 385th (with 1st Scouting Force) Fighter Squadrons
Combat aircraft:	P- 38 (Feb – Jul 44)
	P-51D (from Jul 44)
Stations:	HONINGTON 10 Feb 44 – 3 Nov 45
First Mission:	3 Mar 44 Last Mission: 6 May 45

Distinguished Unit Citation: 27 Dec 44 – Frankfurt, Germany

479th FIGHTER GROUP

'Riddle's Raiders'

Assigned to the Eighth Air Force – May 44

Squadrons:	434th / 435th / 436th Fighter squadrons
Combat aircraft:	P-38 (May – Sep 44)
	P-51D (from Sep 4)
Station:	WATTISHAM 15 May 44 – 22 Nov 45
First Mission:	26 May 44 Last Mission: 25 Apr 45

The last fighter group to join Eighth Air Force Fighter Command, the 479th Fighter Group was also the last group to destroy an enemy aircraft, on 25 Apr 45.

*Some units, or components of units, may have been at other locations on a temporary basis.

The great heavy bombers of the Eighth Air Force could not have survived, nor have been successful, without the fighters that escorted and protected them. It goes without saying that the Eighth's fighter pilots were among the very best of their kind – accumulating a staggering 261 fighter 'Aces'. In total, the Eighth's fighter pilots destroyed over 5,200 German fighters in the air, a further 4,200 were annihilated on the ground by precision strafing attacks.

The roll-call of Eighth Air Force fighter 'Aces', select as it is, nevertheless includes a small, even more elite group – the 27 pilots who destroyed 15 or more enemy aircraft in the air, and another four strafing 'Aces' who destroyed 20 or more aircraft on the ground. Unsurprisingly, their names are among the most famous in the history of military aviation:

Colonel FRANCIS S. 'GABBY' GABRESKI - 56th Fighter Group
Confirmed: 34.4 total / 28 WWII • Probable: 1 / 1 • Damaged: 5 / 3

Major ROBERT S. JOHNSON - 56th Fighter Group
Confirmed: 27 • Damaged: 3

**Major GEORGE E. PREDDY - 352nd Fighter Group
(KIA - 25 Dec 1944)**
Confirmed: 26.833 • Probable: 3 • Damaged: 4

Lt. Colonel JOHN C. MEYER - 352nd Fighter Group
Confirmed: 26 total / 24 WWII • Probable: 1 / 1 • Damaged: 3 / 2

Major RAY S. WETMORE - 359th Fighter Group
Confirmed: 21.25 • Damaged: 1

Lt. Colonel DAVID C. SCHILLING - 56th Fighter Group
Confirmed: 22.5 • Damaged: 6

Major DOMINIC S. GENTILE - 4th Fighter Group
Confirmed: 21.833 • Damaged: 3

Captain FREDERICK J. CHRISTENSEN - 56th Fighter Group
Confirmed: 21.5 • Damaged: 2

Major WALKER H. 'BUD' MAHURIN - 56th Fighter Group
Confirmed: 24.25 total / 20.75 WWII • Probable: 4 / 3
Damaged: 2 / 1

Lt. Colonel GLENN E. DUNCAN - 353rd Fighter Group
Confirmed: 19.5 • Probable: 1 • Damaged: 7

Major DUANE W. BEESON - 4th Fighter Group
Confirmed: 17.333 • Probable: 1 • Damaged: 3

Captain LEONARD K. 'KIT' CARSON - 357th Fighter Group
Confirmed: 18.5 • Damaged: 3

Major WALTER C. BECKHAM - 353rd Fighter Group
Confirmed: 18 • Probable: 2 • Damaged: 4

Major JOHN T. GODFREY - 4th Fighter Group
Confirmed: 16.333 • Probable: 2 • Damaged: 5

Colonel HUBERT 'HUB' ZEMKE - 56th Fighter Group
Confirmed: 17.75 • Probable: 2 • Damaged: 9

Lt. Colonel JOHN B. ENGLAND - 357th Fighter Group
Confirmed: 17.5 • Damaged: 2

Captain JOHN F. THORNELL - 352nd Fighter Group
Confirmed: 17.25 • Damaged: 2

Colonel HENRY W. BROWN - 355th Fighter Group
Confirmed: 14.2 • Damaged: 3

Major ROBERT W. FOY - 357th Fighter Group
Confirmed: 15 • Damaged: 2

Major GERALD W. JOHNSON - 56th Fighter Group
Confirmed: 16.5 • Probable: 1 • Damaged: 4.5

First Lieutenant RALPH K. 'KIDD' HOFER - 4th Fighter Group
Confirmed: 15 • Damaged: 2

Major CLARENCE E. 'BUD' ANDERSON - 357th Fighter Group
Confirmed: 16.25 • Probable: 2 • Damaged: 2

Colonel DONALD J. M. BLAKESLEE - 4th Fighter Group
Confirmed: 14.5 • Probable: 3 • Damaged: 11

Major RICHARD A. PETERSON - 357th Fighter Group
Confirmed: 15.5 • Probable: 1 • Damaged: 2

Captain WILLIAM T. WHISNER - 352nd Fighter Group
Confirmed: 21 total / 15.5 WWII • Probable: 2 / 2 • Damaged: 6 / 0

Lt. Colonel JAMES A. GOODSON - 4th Fighter Group
Confirmed: 14 • Probable: 1 • Damaged: 1

Captain DONALD H. BOCKHAY - 357th Fighter Group
Confirmed: 13.833 • Damaged: 1

And the top four 'Strafing Aces' who each destroyed 20 or more aircraft on the ground:

Lt. Colonel ELWYN G. RIGHETTI - 55th Fighter Group
27 strafing / 7.5 air (†Killed by German civilians 17 Apr 1945)

Captain JOSEPH L. THURY - 339th Fighter Group
25.5 strafing / 3 air

Captain WILLIAM J. CULLERTON - 355th Fighter Group
21 strafing / 5 air

Colonel JOHN D. LANDERS - 55th, 357th & 78th Fighter Groups
20 strafing / 8.5 air, plus 6 in the South-West Pacific

As impressive as the Eighth's long list of fighter Aces is an even longer register of the air gunners who, equipped with their .50-caliber machine-guns, were charged with defending their bombers. Incredibly 305 of these eagle-eyed men each shot down five or more enemy aircraft in their various tours of duty to become 'Aces' in their own right.

FOURTH FIGHTER PATROL | Robert Taylor

*Climbing on full power, P-51s of the Fourth Fighter Group
patrol the skies over northern France ahead of the main force of
Eighth Air Force bombers, 1944.*

THE MIGHTY EIGHTH
SPECIAL GROUPS & SUPPORT UNITS

5th EMERGENCY RESCUE SQUADRON

Established in 8th AF as 65th Fighter Wing Detachment (Air Sea Rescue Sqn)
May 44
Re-designated 5th ERS 26 Jan 45

Combat Aircraft: P- 47D / Catalina OA-10A / B-17G ABL

| Stations: | BOXTED | 1 May 44 – 16 Jan 45 |
| | HALESWORTH | 16 Jan – May 45 |

7th PHOTOGRAPHIC GROUP

Assigned 8th AF 7 Jul 43

Combat aircraft: P-51 F-5 / Spitfire XI / P-51D & K5

| Stations: | MOUNTS FARM | 7 Jul 43 – 22 Mar 45 |
| | CHALGROVE | 22 Mar – Oct 45 |

SPECIAL OPERATIONS GROUP

'The Carpetbaggers'

Established in 8th AF as 801st Bomb Group (P) 28 Mar 44
Re-designated 492nd BOMB GROUP (H) 14 Aug 44

Combat aircraft: B-24 / C-47 / Mosquito XVI / A-26

Stations:	ALCONBURY	4 Dec 43 – Feb 44
	WATTON	7 Feb 44 – 1 Apr 44
	HARRINGTON	8 Mar 44 – 8 Jul 45

Formed to drop weapons, supplies, and agents to the Resistance in enemy occupied countries.

RADIO COUNTER MEASURES SQUADRON

Formed in 8th AF as Radio Counter Measure Detachment 19 Jan 44
Designated 803rd Bomb Squadron (P) 29 Jan 44
Re-designated 36th BOMB SQUADRON (H) B-24 13 Aug 44

Combat Aircraft: B-17 / B-24

Stations:	SCULTHORPE	19 Jan – 16 May 44
	OULTON	16 May – 14 Aug 44
	CHEDDINGTON	14 Aug 44 – 28 Feb 45
	ALCONBURY	28 Feb – 15 Oct 45

NIGHT LEAFLET SQUADRON

Established in 8th AF with 422nd Bomb Squadron 7 Sep 43
Re-designated 858th Bombardment Squadron (H) 28 Jun 44
Re-designated 406 BOMBARDMENT SQUADRON (H) 11 Aug 44

Aircraft:	B-17 / B-24	
Stations:	CHELVESTON	7 Sep 43 – 24 Jun 44
	CHEDDINGTON	24 Jun 44 – 16 Mar 45
	HARRINGTON	16 Mar – 4 Jul 45

Dropped 1,493,760,000 leaflets over Germany and enemy occupied territories

495th FIGHTER TRAINING GROUP

Established in 8th AF 26 Oct 43

Combat Aircraft: P-47 / P-38

| Stations: | ATCHAM | 25 Dec 43 – 15 Feb 45 |
| | CHEDDINGTON | 15 Jan 45 – 21 Mar 45 |

496th FIGHTER TRAINING GROUP

Established in 8th AF 11 Dec 43

Combat Aircraft: P- 38 / P-51

| Stations: | GOXHILL | 27 Dec 43 – 15 Feb 45 |
| | HALESWORTH | 15 Feb 45 – June 45 |

GROUPS THAT ALSO SERVED WITH THE EIGHTH:

1st FIGHTER GROUP

Assigned 8th AF 10 Jun 42
Re-assigned to the 12th AF 14 Sep 42

Aircraft: P-38

3rd PHOTOGRAPHIC GROUP

Assigned 8th AF 5 Sep 42
Re-assigned to the 12th AF Nov 42

Aircraft: P-38 F4 & F5 / B-17

14th FIGHTER GROUP

Assigned 8th AF 18 Aug 42
Re-assigned to the 12th AF 14 Sep 42

Combat aircraft: P-38

15th BOMBARDMENT SQUADRON (L)

Assigned to the 8th AF May 42
Re-assigned to the 12th AF 14 Sep 42

Aircraft: Boston III
Provided the first crew to fly operationally, 29 June 42.

31st FIGHTER GROUP

Assigned to the 8th AF Jun 42
Re-assigned to the 12th AF 14 Sep 42

Aircraft: Mk V Spitfire

52nd FIGHTER GROUP

Assigned to the 8th AF 13 Jul 42
Re-assigned to the 12th AF 14 Sep 42

Aircraft: Mk V Spitfire

60th TROOP CARRIER GROUP

Assigned 8th AF 12 Jun 42
Re-assigned to the 12th AF 14 Sep 42

Aircraft: C-47

62nd TROOP CARRIER GROUP

Assigned 8th AF 6 Sep 42
Re-assigned to the 12th AF 14 Sep 42

Aircraft: C-47 / C-53

64th TROOP CARRIER GROUP

Assigned 8th AF 18 Aug 42
Re-assigned to the 12th AF 14 Sep 42

Aircraft: C-47

67th RECONNAISANCE GROUP

Assigned 8th AF 7 5 Sep 42
Re-assigned to 9th AF Nov 43

Aircraft: Spitfire Vb / L-4 / A-20

82nd FIGHTER GROUP

Assigned to the 8th AF Sep 42
Re-assigned to the 12th AF Dec 42

Aircraft: P-38

97th BOMBARDMENT GROUP (H)

Assigned Eighth AF 20 May 42
Re-assigned to Twelfth AF 14 Sep 42

Aircraft: B-17E & F
Flew the first 8th AF heavy bomber mission from the UK 17 Aug 42

301st BOMBARDMENT GROUP (H)

Assigned Eighth AF 9 Aug 42
Re-assigned Twelfth AF 14 Sep 42

Aircraft: B-17F

315th TROOP CARRIER GROUP

Assigned 8th AF 1 Dec 42
Re-assigned to the 9th AF Oct 43

Aircraft: C-47 / C-53

322nd BOMB GROUP (M)

Assigned Eighth AF 12 Dec 42
Re-assigned Twelfth AF 16 Oct 43

Aircraft: B-26

323rd BOMB GROUP (M)

Assigned Eighth AF 12 May 42
Re-assigned Twelfth AF 16 Oct 43

Aircraft: B-26

350th FIGHTER GROUP

Assigned to the 8th AF 1 Oct 42
Re-assigned to the 12th AF Dec 42

Aircraft: P-40 Airacobra / Spitfire V

358th FIGHTER GROUP

Assigned to the 8th AF 20 Oct 43
Re-assigned to the 9th AF 30 Jan 44

Aircraft: P-47

386th BOMB GROUP (M)

Assigned Eighth AF 4 Jun 43
Re-assigned 9th AF 16 Oct 43

Aircraft: B-26

387th BOMB GROUP (M)

Assigned Eighth AF 25 Jun 43
Re-assigned 9th AF 16 Oct 43

Aircraft: B-26

THE BRAVEST OF THE BRAVE

Only the highest of accolades can be given to the bravery of those who served with the Mighty Eighth and, needless to say, the number of awards earned by its personnel was impressive – 17 Congressional Medals of Honor, 222 Distinguished Service Crosses, 850 Silver Stars, 7000 Purple Hearts and 46,000 Air Medals. But, like all statistics, figures alone can never tell of the many unrecorded acts of heroism, often performed without witness. Of these the world can only surmise but, through the valour of others, can give thanks that such men existed. They were the 'bravest of the brave'.

**MEDAL OF HONOR AWARDS MADE TO EIGHTH
AIR FORCE AIRMEN DURING WORLD WAR II**

18 March 1943   Posthumous †
First Lieutenant JACK W. MATHIS - Bombardier - 303rd Bomb Group

1 May 1943
Sergeant MAYNARD H. SMITH - Gunner - 306th Bomb Group

16 July 1943
Flight Officer JOHN C. MORGAN - Co-pilot - 92nd Bomb Group

1 August 1943
Lt Colonel ADDISON E. BAKER - Group Leader & Co-Pilot - 93rd Bomb Group

1 August 1943   Posthumous †
Second Lieutenant LLOYD H. HUGHES - Pilot - 389th Bomb Group

1 August 1943   Posthumous †
Major JOHN L. JERSTAD - Pilot - 93rd Bomb Group

1 August 1943
Colonel LEON W. JOHNSON - Group Leader & Co-Pilot - 44th Bomb Group

20 December 1943
T/Sergeant FORREST L. VOSLER - Radio Operator - 303rd Bomb Group

20 February 1944
First Lieutenant WILLIAM R. LAWLEY - Pilot - 305th Bomb Group

20 February 1944   Posthumous †
Second Lieutenant WALTER E. TRUEMPER - Navigator - 351st Bomb Group

20 February 1944   Posthumous †
S/Sergeant ARCHIBALD MATHIES - Engineer / Gunner - 351st Bomb Group

11 April 1944
First Lieutenant EDWARD S. MICHAEL - Pilot - 305th Bomb Group

5 June 1944
Lt Colonel LEON R. VANCE - Air Commander - 489th Bomb Group

2 November 1944   Posthumous †
Second Lieutenant ROBERT E. FEMOYER - Navigator - 447th Bomb Group

9 November 1944   Posthumous †
First Lieutenant DONALD J. GOTT - Pilot - 452nd Bomb Group

9 November 1944   Posthumous †
Second Lieutenant WILLIAM E. METZGER - Co-Pilot - 452nd Bomb Group

24 December 1944   Posthumous †
Brigadier General FREDERICK W. CASTLE
Task Force Commander - 4th Bomb Wing

Richard Taylor

Robert Taylor

ACKNOWLEDGEMENTS

CREATED BY THE MILITARY GALLERY

With special thanks to our production team:

Compiled and written by Michael Craig
Production Manager: Craig Smith
Typesetting and Design: Ingrid Hutton

We wish to extend our special thanks to Mark S. Copeland and Michael P. Faley in the production of this title. Both are highly-regarded and respected historians of the Eighth Air Force and currently serve on the Executive Committee and Board of Directors for the 100th Bomb Group Foundation and provided their specialised knowledge to help in the compilation of this book. Mark serves as the chief historical advisor to the Military Gallery on U.S. air combat activities and is a highly-respected consultant to five international war historical museums. He was also a close friend of the late Roger Freeman whose benchmark book on 'The Mighty Eighth' was first published in 1970. We are indebted to Mark's insight and knowledge of the United States Eighth Air Force.

Where not otherwise cited, all other permissions are courtesy of the Military Gallery.

Published by Griffon International Ltd

Printed & Bound in the United Kingdom

Many of the images featured in this book have been reproduced as limited edition prints by the Military Gallery.

www.militarygallery.com

BIBLIOGRAPHY:

Printed:

The Mighty Eighth / Roger Freeman (Arms & Armour Press 1989)

The Mighty Eighth War Manual / Roger Freeman (Cassell 2001)

The Chronological Atlas of World War Two / Charles Messenger (McMillan 1989)

The Army Air Forces In World War II: Combat Chronology, 1941-1945 / Kit Carter & Robert Mueller (The Office Of Air Force History)

Speed Kings / Andy Bull (Random House 2015)

Oil in Germany / Henry Ludmer. (Ohio Journal of Science November 1947)

P-51 Mustangs: Seventy-five Years of America's Most Famous Warbird by Cory Graff (Voyageur Press) – source of Goering quote page XXXX – page number to be added after layouts complete '4 March 1944

At Long Last, A History of the Eighth Air Force / Dr. Kenneth P. Werrell. (Air University Review Jan – Feb 1971)

Bomber Offensive / Arthur Harris (Stoddart 1990)

Online:

www.scottylive.com

www.visitchichester.org

www.boxted-airfield.com